VOLUME 1

THE BASICS

By David A. Lien
Gary Williams

COMPUSOFT® PUBLISHING

A DIVISION OF COMPUSOFT, INC., SAN DIEGO

Contents

Acknowledgments

Editorial Director
Inez Goldberg

Technical Director
Dan Gookin

Production Coordinator
Janice Scanlan

Editors
Dave Waterman
Delanie Alcorn
Jackie Bohan
David Lichty

Cover and Book Design
Masar/Johnston Advertising and Design

Composition Design:
Gary Williams

Illustrations:
Martin Lindsay
Bob Stevens

Project Coordinator
Jerry Kjeldgaard

INTRODUCTION

What Is MS-DOS and What Does It Do?

Before we get into MS-DOS, the Microsoft Disk Operating System, and what it can do, let's take a brief look at what makes the computer itself tick. Don't get nervous; this isn't going to be a technical treatise. Computers are actually pretty simple underneath all the bells and whistles--at least, they operate on a fairly simple principle. Take a moment to run through this with us. It may help answer some questions you have and satisfy your curiosity. You'll have your fingers on the keyboard in no time.

How a Computer Works (More or Less)

You may have heard the expression, "A computer without software is completely dumb." For all practical purposes, this is a true statement. Software is usually thought of as packaged programs with specific tasks, like the SCRIPSIT word processor or the Multiplan spreadsheet, but in fact, software is any information put into the computer. It may be "loaded" from a diskette or typed in at the keyboard, or it may even be permanently "burned" into the computer's memory circuits.

A computer is essentially a passive device. It has all sorts of potential, and it's ready and able to go to work on any information it's given, but it has no "brain" of its own.

It has to be told, for example, to put the cursor on the screen and where to put it. (The cursor is the small flashing light on the screen that indicates where the next character will appear.) It has to be told to make the disks spin and what copyright notice to put on the screen when you first turn it on. In short, it has to be told everything.

First, There's ROM

Some of the information the computer needs just to get up in the morning is permanently embedded in a special place in the internal circuitry called ROM. ROM is *Read-Only Memory* which simply means that all the computer can do is *read* it; it can't change it in any way. How can information be stored permanently in a turned-off electronic device? Here's a gross over-simplification:

Turn the Computer On

You've probably already done this, but if not, be sure the monitor and keyboard are plugged into the computer and that the power cords are all plugged in. Don't worry about putting any disks in the drives yet, just turn the computer and monitor on. In a moment, a copyright notice will appear on the screen.

Get up close to the screen, and look at the individual letters. Notice how they are made up of tiny dots? Each one of those dots is lit up because a certain electronic "switch" is turned on inside the computer. Believe it or not, as complicated and powerful as computers can be, they really only understand two things: on and off. The most awesome software program on the market-- one that would make the computer draw the Mona Lisa or dance a jig--is nothing more than a vast list of on/off instructions. On or off, yes or no, one or zero--in the final analysis, that's really all there is to it.

The memory circuits contain thousands of "switches," and software turns them on and off in a very precise order. So how can the computer do things like put this copyright notice up on the screen without software to flip its switches? Simple; the specific switches required for this job are "welded" in the *on* position at the factory.

As little as possible is put in permanent ROM. The reason for this is twofold: first, the designers want to keep the computer flexible, so that it can be configured to do anything required of it, and second, the memory area needs to be kept free for your data, not cluttered up with housekeeping.

Along Comes MS-DOS

Considerable "housekeeping," or management, however, is required to keep things running (remember, the computer itself, though teeming with potential,

is pretty ignorant...), and that's where MS-DOS, the *Dis*.
comes in. ROM can get the computer organized enoug
"understand" MS-DOS. Once loaded into the computer,
the director whose job is managing the activity going on "in

MS-DOS is itself a program written in a "language" that th
stands and is able to obey. It sends out all the instruction
handling software programs, for directing data from the ke
the screen or printer, and for the host of other functions ne
puter can do more than display its own copyright data.

And Then There's Application Software

The system management capabilities of MS-DOS stay in
memory working even if you remove the MS-DOS disk and
program. If you have a software program that doesn't requi
up" with MS-DOS first, it simply means that the software its
appropriate parts of MS-DOS. The operating system is necessa
be there, one way or another.

But MS-DOS does more than simply keep everything flowing sn
you create documents or other *files* with your application softv
be recorded, or *saved*, onto disk. MS-DOS permits you to mo
around, to make copies of them from disk to disk, to delete the
one to another and so on.

It also makes it possible to prepare diskettes to work on your pa
puter and to make copies of those disks to store for safekeepin
to other operators.

Included on the MS-DOS disk are BASIC, a language for creatin
programs, and Edlin, an easy-to-use editor for writing and editing te

What It Means to Be "In" MS-DOS

We said that MS-DOS is always there in the background, making
example, that when you press the [M] key, an M appears on the s
how do you get it to do all its tricks? When you first start up the

Chapter 1), you'll insert the MS-DOS disk and type in the date and time. Once that's done, a *prompt* will appear on the screen that looks like this:

This prompt means that MS-DOS is ready and at your service. You are at what is called the *command* level. Want to make MS-DOS do tricks? Give commands. That's how it works. The two volumes of this book tell you what all the commands are and what they cause MS-DOS to do.

Once you load a commercial software program, like DeskMate, the MS-DOS A> prompt will go away. This means that, while the system management will still be taken care of, the MS-DOS file and disk handling goodies are no longer available. To take advantage of them, you must return to the MS-DOS command level and to the A> prompt.

The Three Parts of MS-DOS

I. The job of actually operating the system is handled by a part called, appropriately, the System. You can essentially forget about this part of MS-DOS. The commands and instructions in the System are strictly between MS-DOS and the computer and require no participation by you. Once the MS-DOS disk has been put into the computer and you've entered the date and time, the A> prompt appears and the System is loaded into the computer's memory. At this point, you could remove the MS-DOS disk and put it in the closet and close the door if you want. The System will stay in the computer until you turn the power off or press the Reset button.

II. Once the date and time have been entered, some of the simpler MS-DOS functions are also loaded into the computer. Commands to do things like copy and delete files are available even when the MS-DOS disk has been removed. These commands are called *internal* commands because the instructions they require are loaded into the computer's internal memory. All you have to remember about internal commands is that, once loaded at startup time, the MS-DOS disk need not be present to use them. They stay in the computer until it is shut off or reset.

III. More complicated things, like the Edlin line editor and the BASIC programming language, take up too much valuable memory to keep inside at all times, so they are kept on the disk, ready to be loaded when needed. Predictably, the commands that call up these larger programs are called *external* commands. Remember that external commands require the MS-DOS disk to be in the disk drive.

This book will take you through the most basic commands and teach you how to do the things that you're likely to need in your day-to-day use of the computer. From here on, you'll learn by doing.

Have fun!

PART 1

Startup to shutdown

Starting up the System

Startup

Make sure everything is hooked up properly, then turn on your printer and, if you have one, the external hard drive. Now, locate the power switch on your computer. Depending upon which machine you're using, it could be on the back or right up front. Turn on your computer and then the monitor. Next, put the MS-DOS disk, label up, in the bottom drive (the only one if you have a single-drive machine), and close the drive door latch. If nothing happens, or if you see only a "Memory Size" or error message, press the reset button. (On the Tandy 1200 HD, press the [Ctrl] [Alt] and [Del] keys at the same time.)

A faster, more convenient way to do all this is to invest in a power strip and plug everything--your computer and all its peripheral devices--into it. Make it a habit to leave everything turned on and simply use the main switch on the strip for startup and shutdown. Just remember to put the disk in the drive *after* you turned everything on and to remove it *before* you turn everything off. More on this later.

After some copyright information, this message appears:

```
Command v. 2.11
Current date is Tue  1-01-1980
Enter new date:
```

Chapter 1

(If you have a different version of MS-DOS, you may get a slightly different message.)

Setting the date is usually a good idea (so we will), but should you decide not to bother with it in the future, pressing ENTER here will bypass date-setting and move on to time-setting. That can also be bypassed with ENTER if desired.

Setting the Date

Type in today's date. A leading zero is not required for single-digit months or days, and the year can be typed in as two or four digits. Use hyphens, slashes or periods as separators. No need to put in the day of the week; MS-DOS will calculate that, taking into account everything including leap years. The simplest format for a date of January 1, 1986 is probably:

1.1.86 ENTER

This is simplest because it takes advantage of the numeric keypad located on the right side of the keyboard. Notice that this calculator-style "ten-key" pad includes a period key and an ENTER key making the entering of dates a quick, one-hand operation. To use the numeric keypad, press the NUM LOCK key. The small red light on the key will come on once the key's locked, and the keypad will be set to produce numbers. Press the key again to unlock.

Setting the Time

There are occasions, particularly with application programs, when it's useful for the computer to produce the correct time. The ten-key pad can be used to set the time as well:

10.25.55 ENTER

The clock starts when the ENTER key is pressed, so if accuracy is important, set the time a few seconds from now and then press the ENTER key when that precise moment arrives. AM and PM can be handled with 24-hour time; simply use 13 for 1 PM, 14 for 2 PM, etc. Should you make any mistakes in entering the date or time, use the [←] or [BACKSPACE] key to back up. Either key will erase characters as the cursor moves back over them. Then type the correct ones. (Once date and time are set, the clock keeps running until the computer is turned off.

The System Prompt

Pressing [ENTER] after the date and time are set brings up the *SYSTEM PROMPT*. This marker:

A⟩

...indicates that the computer is ready to go.

To display the new date, type **date** [ENTER] when the System prompt appears. Notice that an opportunity to change the date again is being offered. Any time you need to change the date, just type **date** [ENTER] at the System prompt, make the change, and anything dated thereafter by the computer will carry the new date. If there is no need to change the date, just press [ENTER]. Time works the same way; type **time** [ENTER] to see the current time, right down to 1/100 of a second! Type in a new time or press [ENTER] to retain the time displayed, as desired.

SUMMARY

* Turn on the printer and hard drive first, then the computer. Insert the MS-DOS disk in the lower (or only) drive.
* Press [NUM LOCK] to activate the numeric key pad. Use it to set the date and time.
* The System prompt, A⟩, indicates that MS-DOS is ready to go to work.
* Type **date** and **time** to check what date and time have been set on the computer.

CHAPTER 2

The Directory

Entering Commands

You may not realize it, but you just gave MS-DOS two commands. When you typed **date** and **time** at the System prompt, you were telling the computer to do something. Without MS-DOS to tell it how, the computer would have just sat there. A computer without an operating system is pretty helpless. The words date and time mean nothing to the computer itself, but MS-DOS knows that they mean you want it to reset its clock, calculate the day of the week, display the appropriate messages and so on. Asking for the date and time gets right to the heart of what MS-DOS does--giving commands to the computer to tell it what to do and how to do it. Just about all your interaction with MS-DOS from now on will involve commands.

The Directory

Issue MS-DOS another command; this time type **dir** [ENTER]. A long list scrolls up the screen. The list is, in fact, so long that you can't read the first entries before they disappear off the screen. Because it is so long, the list will have to be displayed a "page" at a time. Type the **dir** command again; this time with a short addition that means "give it to me a page at a time":

dir/p [ENTER]

There, the first "page" (screenful) of this list is holding still on the screen.

Only the title scrolled off, and it said:

```
Volume in drive A has no label
Directory of A:
```

The list is a *directory*--a table of contents--of Drive A. (Drive A is the bottom drive in a two-drive system, and the only drive in a one-drive system.) It is a list of all the *files* on the disk in that drive. Since the MS-DOS disk is the disk currently in Drive A, the directory on the screen is naming all the parts of MS-DOS. Let's take a look at it.

The Directory of the MS-DOS Disk

First of all, that title. Volume (meaning the disk) in drive A (the bottom drive) has no label (name). All this means is that no specific name has been given to this directory. Later, when you start creating your own directories and "sub-directories," you'll be assigning them names. For now, it's nothing to worry about.

The first few entries should look something like this:*

```
COMMAND  COM      15957       10-20-84     1:00P
ANSI     SYS       4399       10-20-84     1:00P
CHKDSK   COM       6468       10-20-84     1:00P
DEBUG    COM      12223       10-20-84     1:00P
```

Think of a computer disk as a bookshelf. Collectively, the shelf contains a huge amount of information, but the information is broken down into manageable pieces called books. There are skinny ones, fat ones, technical ones, non-technical ones, and some just for fun. The same applies to the disk. Each "book," or body of information, on a disk is called a file, and the names of all the files on this particular disk are listed in the first column of

---

* Dates, times and sizes (the number to the left of the date) in directories may vary, depending on which computer you are using, and which version of MS-DOS.

the directory on the screen. COMMAND, ANSI, CHKDSK and so on are all file names. By the time you have finished Volume Two in the MS-DOS series, you will have used all of these files to make the computer carry out your instructions.

The second column tells what kind of a file each is, and the third lists the size of the file in "bytes." You've probably heard a lot about bytes and kilobytes and megabytes, but in case you aren't sure what they are, here's a quick simplification: a byte is a character--a letter, number, punctuation mark or space. If a file is 15957 bytes long, it takes up the equivalent of 15957 characters (roughly 2630 six-letter words) on the disk. A Tandy 1000 or 1200 HD floppy disk can hold approximately 360,000 bytes and Tandy hard drives hold from 5 to 70 million bytes, or characters. A kilobyte is a thousand bytes, and a megabyte is a million bytes.

The last two columns tell when (date and time) each file was recorded ("saved") on the disk. Once you begin to put files on your own disks, knowing when each was saved may be important to you.

At the bottom of the screen, there is a message:

```
Strike a key when ready .  .  .
```

If you've seen enough of this part of the MS-DOS directory, press the space bar or any number or letter key and the rest will scroll up. The message at the bottom of the screen now gives the total number of files on this disk and the number of bytes of empty space left (may vary for different versions of MS-DOS):

```
     30 File(s)        59392 bytes free
```

Tandy 2000 users should see:

```
     32 File(s)        299008 bytes free
```

You can obtain a directory of any disk you put into the computer, not just the MS-DOS disk. If you have more than one disk drive or a hard drive, you can see the directory of the disk in any drive by simply specifying the name of the drive. (We'll do that later, when you have something up there to check.) Furthermore, the files on any drive can be subgrouped at your discretion, so that, for example, all your accounting files are in one group and all your word processing files are in another. Each group can have its own "sub-directory," and "sub-sub-directories." This *Tree Structuring* of files is covered in detail in Volume 2.

For the time being, it's only necessary to be able to see what's on a given disk. As a matter of fact, the directory already gives you more information than you probably want to know. There really ought to be a way to display a list of only the names of the files on a disk, without all that other size/date/time stuff to confuse the issue. There is, but first, let's clear the screen.

Clearing the Screen

When you or MS-DOS add something to a full screen, the present contents of the screen scroll up a line at a time to make room at the bottom for the newly added text. The line at the top disappears.

Look about three quarters of the way down the screen. See `Strike a key when ready...?` That was at the bottom of the screen a minute ago. The remainder of the directory ("page 2") was only a few lines, not enough to fill the entire screen, so it just made room for itself at the bottom. In a minute, you'll be calling up another kind of directory, and that will push things up from the bottom as well. To make things less cluttered and to clear the screen of old business before introducing something new, type:

cls ENTER

...at the `A>` prompt. The old directory goes away, and the slate is clean.

To enable the **cls** command on the Tandy 1200 HD, follow these steps:

1. Check the directory of the MS-DOS disk to see if the CONFIG.SYS file is listed. If it is NOT there, type:

   copy con config.sys ENTER
   device = ansi.sys ENTER

If CONFIG.SYS is listed in the MS-DOS directory, type:

copy config.sys + con ENTER
device = ansi.sys ENTER

2. Press Ctrl Z, then ENTER.

3. Reset the computer by pressing Ctrl Alt Del, and you are now ready to use **cls**.

A Names-Only Directory

You added a short extension to the basic **dir** command to make it display one page at a time. There is another extension that makes it display a five-column-wide, all-across-the screen listing of file names only. Type:

dir/w ENTER

In this format, the screen will hold the entire directory of the MS-DOS disk because by leaving out some of the information, it can squeeze five names onto each line. The file type, COM, SYS, EXE, etc., is still included in this format because, as you'll learn a little later, these extensions are actually part of the name.

SUMMARY

* A disk is like a bookshelf; a file is like a book.
* Type **dir** to see a *directory*, or table of contents, of a disk.
* Type **dir/p** to see the directory one "page" at a time.
* Type **dir/w** ("wide directory") to see a names-only directory.
* Type **cls** to clear the screen.
* To enable the **cls** command on the 1200 HD if CONFIG.SYS is on the MS-DOS disk, type **copy config.sys + con** ENTER, then **device = ansi.sys** ENTER. Press Ctrl Z, then ENTER. Reset the computer.
* To enable **cls** on the 1200 HD when CONFIG.SYS is *not* on the MS-DOS disk, type **copy con config.sys** ENTER, then **device = ansi.sys** ENTER. Press Ctrl Z, then ENTER. Reset the computer.

CHAPTER 3

Printing What's on the Screen

There are a couple of ways to print what's on the screen, and as you may have guessed if you studied the keyboard, they both use the [PRINT] key (the [Prt Sc] key on the 1200 HD). To print exactly what's on the screen at this moment (which happens to be the wide version of the directory), press [SHIFT] [PRINT] (or [Shift] [Prt Sc]). If your printer is hooked up and turned on, the wide-format directory should now be on paper. (If your printer is *not* ready, nothing will happen. The screen will freeze, and you won't be able to do anything until you get the printer on line. If you can't do that for some reason, wait a few seconds for the computer to return control to the keyboard or press Reset (or [Ctrl] [Alt] [Del] on the 1200 HD) to cancel the print order. If you reset the computer, use **dir/w** to display the directory again.)

Pressing the [PRINT] key without [SHIFT] produces a slightly different result. Used by itself, the [PRINT] key works as a "toggle" function. That means pressing the key once turns the function on, and pressing it again turns it off. (To toggle the Print function on the 1200 HD, press [Ctrl] [Prt Sc].)

Clear the screen again with **cls** [ENTER], and press [PRINT] ([Ctrl] [Prt Sc] on the 1200 HD) once. Nothing seems to have happened, but now request a regular, long-form directory by typing **dir** [ENTER]. Watch as each line that is fed to the screen is also fed to the printer. Type **cls** [ENTER] again. The screen clears, and if you look at the bottom of the printout, you'll see:

```
A>cls
```

11

...the System prompt and the new command you just typed. As long as the print function is toggled on, everything added to the screen will also be added to the printout. Printing takes place at each "carriage return." Try printing the one-page-at-a-time directory with **dir/p**. As soon as the first page is printed, press ⌈PRINT⌉ to shut off the printer, then any regular key to finish displaying the directory. Up it comes to the screen, but not to the printer.

Halting a Command

Any command that can be typed onto the screen can be stopped in mid-execution with ⌈CTRL⌉ ⌈C⌉. Find the ⌈CTRL⌉ and ⌈C⌉ keys on the keyboard. To do this correctly, you'll need to hold down the ⌈CTRL⌉ key while you tap the ⌈C⌉, then let up on both. For a demonstration, type **dir**, but don't press ⌈ENTER⌉ yet. Get the fingers of your left hand poised over ⌈CTRL⌉ and ⌈C⌉, then press ⌈ENTER⌉ with a finger of your right hand. When four or five lines of the directory have appeared on the screen, press ⌈CTRL⌉ ⌈C⌉ to stop it in its tracks.

Clear the screen and try it again, but this time add the printer. Toggle it on with the ⌈PRINT⌉ key. After a few lines are printed, press ⌈CTRL⌉ ⌈C⌉ to stop the **dir** command. The directory will no longer be sent to either the screen *or* the printer.

⌈CTRL⌉ ⌈C⌉ will not work with ⌈SHIFT⌉ ⌈PRINT⌉ or ⌈Shift⌉ ⌈Prt Sc⌉. Try it. Press ⌈SHIFT⌉ ⌈PRINT⌉, and when printing starts, press ⌈CTRL⌉ ⌈C⌉ to try to stop it. It won't. Just remember that ⌈CTRL⌉ ⌈C⌉ only halts commands you type onto the screen.

SUMMARY

* Press ⌈SHIFT⌉ ⌈PRINT⌉ to print what's on the screen. On the 1200 HD, press ⌈Shift⌉ ⌈Prt Sc⌉.
* Press ⌈PRINT⌉ to turn printer on, press again to turn it off. On the 1200 HD, press ⌈Ctrl⌉ ⌈Prt Sc⌉. With the printer turned on, everything that appears on the screen is printed as it appears.
* Press ⌈CTRL⌉ ⌈C⌉ to halt a command in progress.

CHAPTER 4

Shutting Down the System

In the introduction we attempted to produce analogies to describe MS-DOS. Here's another one: think of MS-DOS as the computer's mother. It wakes the computer up, sends it off to school or work or play, keeps it organized, picks up after it, and at the end of the day, when the work is all done and everything has been put away, the computer returns to Mom and then shuts down for the night. Bet you never thought of it quite like that, but in its own corny way, it's true. MS-DOS should be the one that locks up for the night. When you finish working in some application or another, you shouldn't just hit the Big Switch. You should properly exit the program, get back home to MS-DOS and the A⟩ prompt, remove any floppy disks from their drives and *then* hit the Big Switch.

This last bit about the floppies is pretty important. Since floppy and hard disks are magnetic surfaces on which information is stored by electrical impulses, they are sensitive to BIG electrical impulses. When an electronic device, like a computer, is turned off, it sometimes experiences an internal surge--a jolt of electricity in its circuits. That's perfectly normal and doesn't hurt the computer a bit, but if one of these surge currents should find its way to the sensitive surface of a disk or the recording head while the disk is spinning next to it, damage and/or lost data could result.

Remember this rule: take care of the disks before you touch the power switch. Are there any red lights lit up on the floppy drives? If so, wait until they go out before removing the disks. Is the "Active" light flashing on the hard drive? If so, wait until that goes out before shutting down the hard drive. If the hard drive is built-in or plugged into the main plug strip along with the computer, it's okay to turn both off at the same time. Be sure disk drives are not active *before* the turn-off surge begins.

SUMMARY

* Remove diskettes from drives before turning power off.
* Turn off the hard drive before or at the same time as the computer.

CHAPTER 5

Review of Part One

The intent of Part One was to introduce you to the startup and shutdown procedures for MS-DOS. You've turned the computer on, set the date and time, checked the directory to see what's on the system disk, printed it out, cleared the screen and then shut everything down. You'll do most of these things every time you use the computer, so if anything is not clear, it would be wise to take another run through Part One before you go on.

MS-DOS is at your command. As long as it's not busy doing something else and the system prompt is on the screen with a flashing cursor, you can issue commands. You've learned some commands already, and you'll be learning many more as you proceed through this volume and the next. Some commands are carried out by the MS-DOS "system" itself. These tend to be the shorter, simpler ones; **date**, **cls** and **dir** are examples. Beginning with the next chapter, we'll begin to look at some commands that are complicated enough to require a whole file full of instructions to the computer. They won't be complicated to you, however; you'll just have to type in the command. What MS-DOS has to go through to execute the command is its problem!

As we mentioned in the Introduction, commands that MS-DOS can handle immediately, without loading one of the files on the disk, are called *internal* commands. Commands which require MS-DOS to open one of its files--from the directory of MS-DOS programs we've been working with--are called *external* commands. It won't really matter much to you right now whether a particular command is internal or external, as long as it gets the job done.

Command Review

date displays current date and offers the opportunity to change date. Change can be bypassed with ⌈ENTER⌉.

time displays current time and offers the opportunity to change time. Change can be bypassed with ⌈ENTER⌉.

dir displays "table of contents" of a disk. Continues scrolling until bottom of directory appears on screen.

dir/p stops display of directory when screen is full. When finished reading first "page" of directory, press any number or letter key to see next page.

dir/w displays "wide" version of directory. Includes only names of files and their extensions in five columns across screen.

cls clears screen, leaving only system prompt. **cls** must be enabled on the Tandy 1200 HD before it can be used.

Keyboard Commands

⌈CTRL⌉ ⌈C⌉ stops execution of a typed command.

⌈PRINT⌉ (⌈Ctrl⌉ ⌈Prt Sc⌉ on the 1200 HD) toggles on/off. Sends everything *going to* the screen also to the printer.

⌈SHIFT⌉ ⌈PRINT⌉ (⌈Shift⌉ ⌈Prt Sc⌉ on the 1200 HD) sends everything *currently on* the screen to the printer. Commonly called a *screen dump*.

Notes

Startup Turn on computer, then insert the MS-DOS disk in bottom drive (Drive A).

Turn on hard drive before, or with same switch as, computer.

Shutdown Remove disks and shut down hard drive before turning off computer. Hard drive can be shut off with same switch as computer.

P A R T   2

Using MS-DOS to prepare your diskettes

CHAPTER 6

Disk Drives

The Great Compatibility Question

Because this book covers three Tandy computers, it might be appropriate to take a moment to sort out "who's on first." Generally speaking, the 1000 and 1200 HD are "compatible" with the IBM PC. This means that software that runs on the IBM will usually run on these two machines.

The Tandy 2000 is different from the rest because it's a much more powerful machine. Its floppy disks can store twice as much data, and it "computes" twice as fast.

Disk Capacities

In Chapter 2 we described a byte as the memory required to store one character--a letter, number, space or punctuation mark. The amount of memory that came with your computer, 256K, 512K and so on refers to the quantity of characters that can be loaded into the computer *at any one time*.

Suppose you have a 256K machine, and you want to run a spreadsheet program which requires 56K of memory. The spreadsheet program itself--all the instructions to the computer, the calculations, the screen formats--all this structure uses up the equivalent of 56 thousand characters, and they all need to be in the computer at once.

Having 256K capacity means that you can now put up to 200 thousand num-

19

bers and letters of your own data into the spreadsheet. If any one of your spreadsheet projects--your profit/loss statement, your checking account ledger or whatever--gets bigger than 200 thousand characters, you'll need more memory.

This *volatile*, or *Random Access Memory* (RAM), is not the same as *disk* memory. Once you are finished with your profit/loss statement, for example, you can "save" it onto a disk--permanently record it for future use--and then *clear it out of the computer*, freeing up 200K for the next project, or freeing up all 256K if you also clear out the spreadsheet program itself.

While the computer can only work on 256K at any one time, the total amount of data you can have on hand and ready to load up is limited only by the storage capacity of a disk, multiplied by the number of disks you have. In the case of floppy disks, of course, this number is potentially infinite.

The Tandy 1000 and 1200 HD floppy drives are capable of storing approximately 360K on each disk. Once a disk is full, out it comes; inserting a fresh one provides another 360K. Because the 2000 is capable of packing the data more tightly onto the disk, a floppy in that machine can hold up to 720K. All three computers use "double-sided" diskettes. Data is stored on both sides of the disk, however it's done automatically--you don't have to turn the disk over or do anything else.

If you have a hard drive, your disk isn't removable, but depending on the model, its total capacity will be from 10 to 70 million characters. How much is that? Counting every space and punctuation mark, a typical typewritten page is about 3K (3000) characters. Ten million divided by 3K = 3333 pages. After that, you'll need to add a secondary hard drive.

SUMMARY

* Tandy 1000 and 1200 HD are "IBM compatible."
* Tandy 2000 has twice the disk capacity and works at double the speed.
* RAM (Random Access Memory) is the amount of data that can be in the computer at one time.
* When work is finished on a file, it can be stored on a disk, then cleared out of RAM.
* Total disk storage capacity is limited only by the number of available disks.

Formatting a Floppy Disk

The Format Command

Before any disk, floppy or hard, can be used to store data, it must be prepared by the computer. This preparation is called *formatting*. Floppy diskettes are formatted with another MS-DOS command: **format**. Formatting the hard drive is a little different; it's covered in Chapter 8. (If you don't have a hard drive, you can skip Chapter 8, and we'll pick you up in Chapter 9.)

Start up the computer again or, if it's already on, press the reset button (or Ctrl Alt Del). Insert the MS-DOS disk in the bottom drive (Drive A) and a blank disk, right out of the box, in the top drive (Drive B). Be sure the labels on both disks are up and out.

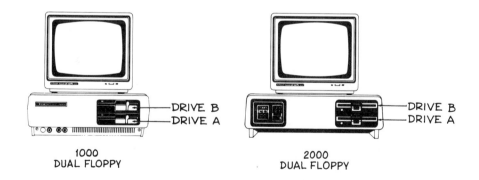

Figure 7-1

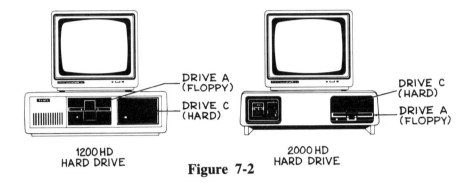

DRIVE A (FLOPPY)
DRIVE C (HARD)

DRIVE C (HARD)
DRIVE A (FLOPPY)

1200 HD HARD DRIVE

2000 HD HARD DRIVE

Figure 7-2

Type the date and time. Once the A⟩ system prompt appears, type the command:

format b: ⟨ENTER⟩

The **b:** at the end of the command tells MS-DOS that the diskette you want to format is in Drive B.

One-Drive Systems

If you have a single-drive system, just type the **format** command without adding **b:**. For the rest of this chapter, when we specify adding **b:**, ignore us. The computer will prompt you to:

```
Insert new diskette for drive A:
and strike any key when ready
```

Tandy 1200 HD users will see:

```
Insert new diskette for drive A:
and press any key when ready
```

Remove the MS-DOS disk, and insert a blank disk.

This is one of those "external" commands we mentioned that require MS-DOS to go to the disk and dip into one of its files. As soon as you give the command, the MS-DOS disk spins and a copyright notice appears. This indicates that the **format** command requires a program to accomplish its task, and if you glance at your printout of the directory, you'll see the FORMAT program listed. An instruction appears on the screen:

```
Insert new diskette for drive B:
and strike any key when ready
```

You've already inserted a new diskette in Drive B, so press any key.

By the way, "strike any key", which appears now and then in MS-DOS, is not strictly correct. Certain keys, like the [SHIFT] key and a couple of others, won't work for this. In practice, most people just tap the space bar.

On the 1000 and 2000 you are treated to a little graphic display to prove that FORMAT is actually working. What it's doing is creating magnetic "tracks" on the disk, similar to phonograph-record tracks, and every time it creates another track, it checks it off on the screen. When the job is done, a message like this appears:

```
Format complete

    362496 bytes total disk space
    362496 bytes available on disk

Format another (Y/N)?
```

The 362496 is the "360 K" we mentioned as the capacity of Tandy 1000 and 1200 HD diskettes. You Tandy 2000 users will see `731136 bytes`.

Go ahead and press [N] for "no" and we'll try one a slightly different way. Insert another new disk, and at the `A>` prompt, type:

format/v b: [ENTER] (Single floppy users just type **format/v.**)

Everything proceeds as above, but when the formatting is done, this message appears:

```
Volume label (11 characters, ENTER for none)?
```

Remember when we were looking at the directory in Chapter 1 and we encountered the message Volume in drive A has no label? That meant that the disk had no name. Now, during formatting of a new disk the opportunity is being presented to give this one a name. Type:

SAMPLE_DISK [ENTER]

That completes the formatting process, and Format another (Y/N)? appears on the screen. This new disk is now named SAMPLE_DISK. Press [N] and check the directory to see the disk name. Type:

dir b: [ENTER]

Don't worry about that File not found message. It didn't list any files because there aren't any yet.

Take the formatted disk out, and prepare a label for it. It might be helpful to make a mark on the label to indicate that this disk is already formatted, so you won't get confused. Do this before affixing the label. An alternative would be to set up a special box for formatted blank diskettes.

Insert another new one, and type the **format** command to start the formatting process again. The Format another (Y/N)? message appears after each disk is formatted, and you can keep going as long as you like. When you're tired of formatting, press [N] to return to the system prompt.

Bad Tracks

Once in a while, you'll get a bum diskette. For one reason or another, it will have a bad spot or two which won't format. This doesn't happen nearly as much as it used to because of the generally improved quality of today's diskettes, but should MS-DOS encounter a stubborn place, it will skip over it and format the rest of the disk. This means that the disk won't hold quite as much data, but it's still usable.

During formatting the screen display will look something like this if an area that can't be formatted is encountered on the disk:

```
Formatting tracks
++++++++++++++++++++++++++++++++++?+++++++++

      362496 bytes total disk space
        5120 bytes in bad sectors
      357376 bytes available on disk
```

Tandy 1200 HD users will simply be shown the number of bytes of total disk space, in bad sectors and available on disk.

The diskette will operate just like any other, but won't have the same capacity. It often works to format the same diskette a second time. In many cases the formatting will "take" on the second or third try; however if you're not in desperate need of the diskette, it's probably better to put it aside and take it back to the dealer.

SUMMARY

* Preparing a disk to store data is called *formatting*.
* To format a disk in Drive B, type **format b:**.
* Typing **format/v** provides an opportunity to name a diskette.
* If MS-DOS encounters a bad spot on a diskette, it will format "around" it, but it's a good idea to replace the disk if possible.

CHAPTER 8

Formatting the Hard Drive

If you don't have a hard drive, skip ahead to Chapter 9.

A hard drive changes your life somewhat, but it doesn't entirely replace the floppy disk drive. You'll still need the floppy drive to introduce new software, to make backups of the hard drive (vitally important, and covered in Chapter 11), and to make "portable" copies of your files to carry to other computers. All the information in this book relating to floppies is important to you.

We mention this because, once you get the hard drive formatted, MS-DOS will be put on it along with your software programs and probably all of your files. It's easy to forget the need for floppies once you get rolling with a hard drive.

One Big Note for Hard Drive Users

The hard drive is Drive C. (The floppies, if you have two, are A and B, and should you add a second hard drive, it would be D.) Once MS-DOS is put on the hard drive, you'll be making Drive C the *active* or default drive. This means that from this point forward *your default system prompt will be* C>. Throughout the rest of the book, when we refer to the A> prompt, you'll see the hard drive prompt, C>.

If this complicates things for you at all (you'll quickly get used to it), you'll be compensated by the fact that you don't normally have to bother with drive designators at all. In other words, while floppy users are busy attaching **b:**

to their file names and **a:** to the MS-DOS files, you'll be able to relax in the knowledge that everything you have is on the same drive. You won't have to worry about whether a command is *internal* or *external*, because MS-DOS and all of its programs are present at all times.

FORMATTING THE TANDY 1000 HARD DRIVE

If your hard drive is not built in, be sure that it's hooked up according to the instructions that came with it. Before turning on an external hard drive or a computer with a built-in hard drive, turn it upside down and locate the *Media Error Map* on the bottom. (DON'T ever turn the hard drive upside down while it's on.) Copy any numbers you find on the map to a piece of scratch paper and save it for later.

If they are not connected to a common switch, first turn on the hard drive, then the computer. Tandy recommends that you wait about 30 minutes for the hard drive to warm up before beginning the formatting procedure. This doesn't apply to normal use of the drive, just formatting.

Put the MS-DOS disk in Drive A and reset the computer. Enter the date and time as usual, and at the A> prompt, remove the MS-DOS disk and insert the **Hard Disk Utilities** diskette that came with your hard drive. Type the first command:

hsect [ENTER]

The message will appear to:

Press any key to begin formatting drive C

Press the space bar and the first phase begins. MS-DOS will inform you that it is Formatting ..... and in a few minutes (two or three minutes for a 10-meg drive, around six minutes for a 15 meg) it will say Format completed!. Don't get too excited, however, you're not finished yet.

Initializing the Hard Drive

Phase two of the procedure requires another command. When the Format completed! message appears and the A> prompt returns, type:

fdisk [ENTER]

The initialization Main Menu appears:

```
FDISK Options

Current Hard Disk Drive: 1

Choose one of the following:

          1.         Create DOS Partition
          2.         Change Active Partition
          3.         Delete DOS Partition
          4.         Display Partition Data
          5.         Select Next Hard Disk Drive
          6.         Select Previous Hard Disk Drive

Enter Selection -->

Press ESC to exit to MS-DOS
```

Press [1] to Create DOS Partition. The next message is:

```
Create Dos Partition

Current Hard Disk Drive: 1

Do you wish to use the entire hard disk for DOS (Y/N) --> Y
```

It's asking if you want to break the hard disk up into sections for special applications, or use the entire thing for MS-DOS and MS-DOS files. You only want one partition for now, so press [Y].

The Main Menu appears again; this time press [4]:

```
          4.         Display Partition Data
```

```
Current Hard Disk Drive: 1

Partition      Status     Type      Start      End       Size
    1            N        DOS         0        304       305

Total Hard disk space is 305 cylinders

Press any key to continue --------------->
```

This report tells you, briefly, that Partition number 1 is a "non-active" (we'll come back to that) partition, that it is configured for MS-DOS, that it starts at cylinder 0 and extends to cylinder 304. Partition 1 uses 305 out of a total disk space of 305 cylinders. In other words, it takes up the whole disk.

The Status is the only thing we want to change. Non-active means that this is not the drive that the computer will automatically go to for instructions at boot-up time. You remember that you can change the default drive any time you want to by just typing its number and a colon, but when you reset or turn the power on, MS-DOS always returns to Drive A and the A> prompt.

By changing the status of the hard drive to Active, guess what you're doing? You're fixing it so that the computer will boot up from the hard drive and automatically display the C> prompt. As we said at the beginning of this chapter, you'll be reading A> through the rest of this book, but on your screen, you'll be seeing C>. In just a moment, we're going to copy the MS-DOS diskette onto the hard drive, and after that, you won't need to use the MS-DOS floppy diskette at all. You can put it away in the cupboard.

Making the Hard Drive the Active Drive

So. On to changing the status. Press the space bar to get out of the status report and back into the Main Menu. Press [2] to change the active partition:

```
   2.          Change Active Partition
```

The status report reappears, along with the instruction:

```
Enter the number you want to make active
```

You only have one partition, and its number is 1, so press ①. Once again the menu; check the status one more time to see if the one-and-only partition has been changed to active. Do that by selecting item 4 on the Main Menu:

```
4,          Display Partition Data
```

Back comes the status report, and sure enough, Status is now changed to A:

```
Partition    Status    Type     Start     End      Size
    1           A       DOS        0       304      305
```

Press the space bar to get back to the Main Menu, then [ESC] to return to MS-DOS. A short beep and a message will tell you that:

```
System needs to reboot
Insert system disk in Drive A
Please reset the system
```

Put the MS-DOS diskette back in Drive A and press the reset button.

Enter the date and time again, then remove the MS-DOS diskette and put the Hard Disk Utilities diskette back in the drive.

Finishing the Format Procedure

This may seem like a long process, but luckily, with a hard drive, you normally only have to do it once.

The next command prepares the disk to receive MS-DOS. Type:

hformat c: /b/s/v [ENTER]

The message on the screen is:

```
Insert DOS diskette in drive A:
and strike any key when ready
```

After replacing the utility disk with the DOS disk, press the space bar. The computer displays:

```
Enter next head, track pair or press <ENTER> to quit,
```

If your *Media Error Map* did not list any numbers, simply press [ENTER] to start the Format procedure. If, however, one or more Head and Cylinder error numbers were listed now is the time to report them to the computer (did you remember to jot them down earlier?). For example, if your listing showed:

```
    Head        Cylinder
     1            282
```

you should type in the numbers:

1,282 [ENTER]

Do this for each set of numbers that are listed on the Media Error Map. After the last pair of numbers are entered, press [ENTER]. (Most hard disks have one or more small bad spots on the disk. This is normal, and the manufacturer identifies the locations of these spots and writes them on the "Map" on the bottom of the disk drive. When you enter the locations now, you are telling MS-DOS to format around them. Aside from a minute loss of storage capacity, the hard drive will operate as though the spots didn't even exist.)

Again, we are prompted to:

```
Press any key to begin formatting C:
```

Not the most appropriate message, since you already formatted Drive C once, but it's now going through a final phase of the formatting, so press the space bar to get it started. For this part of the format, a display is provided to keep you amused while you wait:

```
Formatting Cylinders...
 + + + + + + + +-------------------------------------------------
-----------------------------------------------------------------
--------------- ...etc.
```

When finished, this message appears:

```
System transferred
Volume label (11 characters, ENTER for none)?
```

The format is complete, and the MS-DOS system is transferred to the hard drive. Now, how about a name for the hard disk? Type:

Hard_Disk [ENTER]

That seems appropriate. And at last:

```
Format complete
    10592256 bytes total disk space
       45056 bytes used by system
    10547200 bytes available on disk
```

Copying the MS-DOS Programs to the Hard Disk

All that remains is to copy the rest of the MS-DOS disk to the new Drive C. The **copy** command does the trick. Type:

copy a:*.* c: [ENTER]

This copies all files to the hard drive, and the job is done. When the copy is complete, remove the floppies and press the reset button or shut off the computer and turn it back on again. The `C>` prompt should automatically appear, and you're in business.

FORMATTING THE TANDY 2000 HARD DRIVE

If your hard drive is not built in, be sure that it's hooked up according to the instructions that came with it. Before turning on an external hard drive or a computer with a built-in hard drive, turn it upside down and locate the *Media Error Map* on the bottom. (DON'T ever turn the hard drive upside down while it's on.) Copy any numbers you find on the map to a piece of scratch paper and save it for later.

If they are not connected to a common switch, first turn on the hard drive, then the computer. Tandy recommends that you wait about 30 minutes for the hard drive to warm up before beginning the formatting procedure. This doesn't apply to normal use of the drive, just formatting.

Put the MS-DOS disk in Drive A and reset the computer. Enter the date and time as usual, and at the A> prompt, type the first command:

confighd [ENTER]

The copyright notice appears, along with the following message:

```
Enter next head, track pair or press <ENTER> to quit.
```

The Media Error Map

Enter the Head and Track numbers from the *Media Error Map* attached to the bottom of the computer or external drive. (DON'T turn the computer or drive upside down while it's running! Check the list you made earlier.) For example

3,276 [ENTER]
2,170 [ENTER]

Press [ENTER] again when the last Head/Track number has been entered or press [ENTER] if the *Media Error Map* is blank.

Starting the Formatting

The computer then asks you to:

```
Press any key to begin formatting C:
```

Press the space bar and watch the display as each cylinder is formatted.

```
Formatting cylinders
```

```
+ + +-------------------------------------------------
------------------------------------------------------
----------------- ...etc.
```

When finished, this message appears:

```
Format complete

10616832 bytes total disk space
73278 bytes used by system
10543104 bytes available on disk

32 files are copied from the DOS disk to Drive C
```

The hard drive is now formatted, and MS-DOS (all 32 files of it) has been copied over to it. Your "active" drive is now Drive C--the hard drive. Whenever you turn on or reset the computer, control will automatically go to Drive C, and the C> prompt will appear. You can remove the MS-DOS floppy disk from Drive A and put it away.

FORMATTING THE TANDY 1200 HARD DRIVE

Make sure the computer is turned off, then tip it over and locate the *Media Error Map* on the bottom. Copy any numbers you find on the map to a piece of scratch paper and save it for later.

Turn the computer on, and after it completes the RAM test, put the MS-DOS disk in Drive A, and enter the date and time as usual. At the A> prompt, type the first command:

llfdfmt [ENTER]

MS-DOS will warn us that:

```
ALL DATA on the fixed disk will be DESTROYED
Do you want to continue (y or n) ?
```

The format procedure erases all data that may have been previously stored on the hard drive. At this point, we haven't used the hard drive yet so there is no data to lose. Answer the question by typing:

y

The next question is:

```
Which fixed disk to format (C or D) ?
```

As discussed earlier, the hard drive is normally designated as Drive C so answer the question by typing:

c

The message:

```
Press any key when ready (Ctrl-Break to abort)
```

will appear.

Press the space bar, and the first phase begins. MS-DOS will inform you that it is:

```
Formatting fixed disk  c: allow one hour for completion
```

In about 30 minutes the first phase of the procedure will be complete, and MS-DOS will report:

```
Format complete, no areas deleted

Are there any areas to manually delete ? (y or n)
```

If your *Media Error Map* did not list any numbers, answer by typing **n**. If, however, one or more Head and Cylinder error numbers were listed now is the time to report them to the computer (did you remember to jot them down earlier?). Type **y** and enter the numbers under the appropriate headings. For example:

```
Head          Cylinder      Degree      Enter 'd' if last
entry
  1             126           339
```

Press ENTER after entering each number. If your hard drive has more than one Media Error listing, press ENTER twice to move to the next line. Do this for each set of numbers that are listed on the Media Error Map. After the last set of numbers are entered, type **d** (you must use lower case) and see the message:

```
Format complete, returning to DOS.
```

Don't get too excited however, you're not finished yet.

Partitioning the Hard Drive

Phase two of the procedure requires another command. When the A> prompt returns, type:

part ENTER

The PARTition Menu appears:

```
PART Options
Choose one of the following:

         1.       Display Partition Data
         2.       Change Active Partition
         3.       Delete DOS Partition
         4.       Create DOS Partition

Enter choice:  [1]

Enter ESC to exit to DOS
```

Ignore the default entry [1] provided by the computer and press [4] ENTER to Create DOS Partition. The next message is:

```
Create DOS Partition

Do you wish to use the entire
Winchester disk for DOS (Y/N)? [Y]
```

It's asking if you want to break the hard disk up into sections for special applications, or use the entire thing for MS-DOS and MS-DOS files. You only want one partition for now, so press [ENTER] to accept the [Y] default answer.

The DOS Partition report appears:

```
Create DOS Partition


Partition Status   Type  Start End   Size
     1        A     DOS    0    304   305

Total Hard disk space is 305 cylinders



Enter ESC to return to Menu
```

This report tells you, briefly, that Partition number 1 is an "Active" partition, that it is configured for MS-DOS, that it starts at cylinder 0 and extends to cylinder 304. Partition 1 uses 305 out of a total disk space of 305 cylinders. In other words, it takes up the whole disk.

Press [Esc] to return to the PARTition Menu, then press [Esc] again to see the message:

```
System must now be Rebooted
Insert a DOS diskette in Drive A:
and strike any key

( If you are using PREPARE, you must
  reload it after reboot to complete
  the hard drive installation. )
```

With the MS-DOS diskette still in Drive A, press the space bar to return to MS-DOS.

Enter the date and time again.

Finishing the Format Procedure

This may seem like a long process, but luckily, with a hard drive, you normally only have to do it once.

The next command prepares the disk to receive MS-DOS. Type:

format c: /s/f [ENTER]

The message on the screen is:

```
Press any key to begin formatting fixed disk C:
```

Not the most appropriate message, since you already formatted Drive C once, but it's now going through a final phase of the formatting, so press the space bar to get it started.

```
Formatting drive C: ....
```

This procedure takes about 2 minutes. And at last, this message:

```
Format Complete
System transferred

 10593280 bytes total disk space
    42162 bytes in system files
 10551118 bytes available on disk
```

Copying the MS-DOS Programs to the Hard Disk

All that remains is to copy the rest of the MS-DOS disk to the new Drive C. The **copy** command does the trick. Type:

copy a:*.* c: [ENTER]

This copies all files to the hard drive.

Switch the default drive to C by typing:

c: [ENTER]

The C⟩ prompt should automatically appear, and you're in business.

* Your active drive will now be the hard drive, Drive C.

* When the book refers to the A⟩ prompt, you will generally see the C⟩ prompt.

FORMATTING THE TANDY 1000 HARD DRIVE

1. Copy the numbers from the *Media Error Map* on the bottom of the computer or external drive. Do this with the power off.
2. At the A⟩ prompt, replace MS-DOS disk with Hard Disk Utilities diskette.
3. Type **hsect** [ENTER].
4. Press the space bar.
5. When the A⟩ prompt returns, type **fdisk** [ENTER].
6. Press [1] to create DOS partition.
7. Press [Y] to use entire hard disk for MS-DOS.
8. Press [2] to change the active partition.
9. Press [1] to make partition 1 active.
10. Press [4] to check status.
11. Press the space bar to return to the Main Menu.
12. Press [ESC] to return to MS-DOS.
13. Replace the utilities disk in Drive A with the MS-DOS disk, and press the reset button.
14. Enter date and time, then switch disks again.
15. Type **hformat c: /b/s/v** [ENTER].
16. Switch disks once more, and press the space bar.
17. Press [ENTER] if there were no media errors. If there were errors, enter the Head and Cylinder numbers copied from the map (step 1).
18. Press [ENTER] after each head/cylinder pair.
19. Press [ENTER] again after all errors are entered.
20. Press the space bar to complete formatting.
21. When prompted, type **Hard_Disk** to give name to the drive.
22. With the MS-DOS disk still in Drive A, type **copy a:*.* c:** [ENTER].
23. Remove floppies and press the reset button to bring up the C⟩ prompt.

FORMATTING THE TANDY 2000 HARD DRIVE

1. Copy the numbers from the *Media Error Map* on the bottom of the computer or external drive. Do this with the power off.
2. At the A> prompt, type **confighd** [ENTER].
3. Press [ENTER] if there were no media errors.
4. If there were errors, enter the Head and Track numbers copied from the map (step 1).
5. Press [ENTER] after each head/track pair.
6. Press [ENTER] again after all errors are entered.
7. Press the space bar to start formatting.
8. Remove the MS-DOS disk, and press the reset button to bring up the C> prompt.

FORMATTING THE TANDY 1200 HARD DRIVE

1. Copy the numbers from the *Media Error Map* on the bottom of the computer or external drive. Do this with the power off.
2. At the A> prompt, type **llfdfmt** [ENTER].
3. Press [Y] to start formatting.
4. Press [C] to select Drive C.
5. Press the space bar to start phase one.
6. Press [N] if there were no media errors and go to step 10.
7. Press [Y] if there errors. Enter the Head, Cylinder and Degree numbers copied from the map (step 1).
8. Press [ENTER] after each head/cylinder/degree entry.
9. Press [ENTER] twice after typing in the degree number if there is more than one media error to enter.
10. Type **d** after all errors are entered.
11. At the A> prompt, type **part** [ENTER].
12. Press [4] [ENTER] to create DOS partition.
13. Press [ENTER] to accept the [Y] default.
14. Press [Esc] twice and then the space bar to return to MS-DOS.
15. Enter the date and time.
16. Type **format c: /s/f** [ENTER] to complete the format procedure.
17. Press the space bar to start the last phase.
18. Type **copy a:*.* c:** [ENTER] to copy all files to the hard disk.
19. Type **c:** [ENTER] to bring up C> prompt.

CHAPTER 9

Disk Protection

Diskettes are somewhat fragile for a couple of reasons: one, because information is stored on them by magnetic impulses and two, because, unlike your favorite stereo tapes, every little "impulse" counts. You'd probably never notice the loss of one or two notes of music from a tape, but if one or two of the wrong bytes on a computer disk get erased or changed, the entire program could be rendered useless. The damaged characters may be in the instructions that make the program run, and a computer won't ad-lib; if a detailed instruction is missing one or two characters, it usually just won't work.

Generally speaking, a diskette is protected from damage by things you type at the keyboard if there's a small adhesive strip called a *write-protect tab* covering the notch in the side of the disk. (See fig. 9-1)

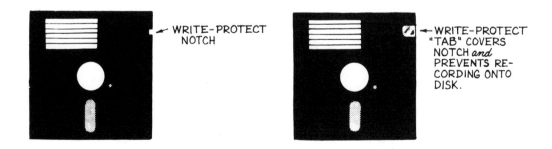

WRITE–PROTECT NOTCH

WRITE–PROTECT "TAB" COVERS NOTCH *and* PREVENTS RECORDING ONTO DISK.

Figure 9-1

Some external hard drives are protected with a red button on the front panel (See fig. 9-2). Press the button and it lights up, indicating that information can be *read* from the hard drive, but no new information can be *written to* it. Press the button again to turn protection off. Built-in hard drives do not have write protection.

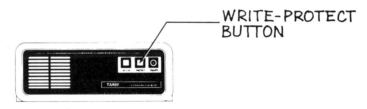

WRITE-PROTECT
BUTTON

Figure 9-2

A write-protect tab or switch prevents any new information from being saved onto the disk. The MS-DOS disk should wear one at all times. Data diskettes, on the other hand, should not have tabs installed because you will *want* to save data on them. While a write-protect tab can protect a disk from being recorded over, it doesn't protect it from other kinds of damage, so a copy, or "backup," should be made of all important disks.

SUMMARY

* A write-protect tab prevents the computer from saving (recording) anything new on the diskette. Existing contents are protected from erasure and over-writing.
* Some external hard drives use a red button for protection. Internal hard drives are not write protected.
* A protected disk can be read from, but not written to.

CHAPTER 10

Making Copies of Floppy Disks

NOTE TO HARD DRIVE USERS: Although your chapter is Chapter 11, it wouldn't be a bad idea for you to run through this as though you didn't have a hard drive. There will undoubtedly be times when you'll want to copy floppy-to-floppy, so you should know how. If you need to change your prompt back to A>, type **a:** ENTER and try this chapter with us.

Copying the MS-DOS Diskette

The very first thing you'll want to do with one of your newly-formatted diskettes is make a duplicate copy of the MS-DOS disk. Once copied, this duplicate should become your working copy of MS-DOS. The original should be stored away in a safe place and only used again to make a new working copy should something happen to the first.

With the write-protected MS-DOS disk in Drive A, a formatted diskette in Drive B (no tab on this one) and the A> system prompt on the screen, type:

diskcopy a: b: ENTER (The spaces after the command and after the **a:** are mandatory.)

MS-DOS advises you to:

```
Insert source diskette in drive A:
Insert formatted target diskette in drive B:
Strike any key when ready
```

One-Drive System

Since you don't have two drives, there is no need to specify any; simply type **diskcopy** [ENTER], and the following prompt from MS-DOS appears:

```
Insert formatted target diskette in drive A:
Strike any key when ready.
```

The disks are already inserted, so tap the space bar. The computer reports that it is:

```
Copying...
```

and in a moment...

```
Copy complete
```

```
Copy another (Y/N)?
```

Press [N] to return to the A> prompt. MS-DOS copies everything from the disk in Drive A to the disk in Drive B, resulting in two identical disks. Now you can put the original away, and use the copy in your day-to-day operations. The new working copy should also be treated to a write-protect tab.

One-Drive System

Making duplicate disks with a single disk drive necessitates some disk swapping. You may have noticed that shortly after you inserted the formatted target disk in your one-and-only floppy drive, a new prompt appeared:

```
Insert source diskette in drive A:
Strike any key when ready
```

MS-DOS will ask you to insert first one disk, then the other for a while as it "memorizes" a block of data from the source disk, then records it onto the target disk. Remember that a disk usually holds more than the computer itself can hold (RAM memory), so a single-drive diskcopy must be done in stages.

Copying a Data Disk

A data disk (one that contains information created by you) is copied with the same command (**diskcopy**) and the same procedure as required for copying the MS-DOS disk. The only difference is that when prompted to `Insert source disk`, you must remove the MS-DOS disk and insert the disk you want copied. The target disk is still a blank, formatted disk. We haven't put anything on a data disk yet, so we'll hold off copying one until we have something interesting to copy.

Checking a Diskette's Name, or "Volume Label"

The command to check the name of a disk is **vol**. The MS-DOS disk has no name, and if you type **vol a:** you'll see the message you've seen before:

`Volume in drive A has no label`

Put the formatted disk you named "SAMPLE_DISK" in Drive B (or replace the MS-DOS disk in Drive A, if you only have one drive) and type:

vol b: `ENTER` (just **vol** `ENTER` if you have one drive...)

Now the name appears. If you have multiple drives or a hard disk, this is a handy way to check which disk is where. Once a disk is named, it can't be renamed unless it is reformatted. Since reformatting will erase the contents of the disk, it really becomes a new disk, with a new name.

SUMMARY

* The original MS-DOS disk should be kept in a safe place. Use copies for day-to-day operation.
* Type **diskcopy a: b:** to copy the disk in Drive A onto a formatted blank disk in Drive B. (Single floppy drive users type only **diskcopy**.)
* Copy data diskettes the same way as the MS-DOS disk, except, when prompted to do so, remove the MS-DOS disk and insert the disk you want to copy.
* Type **vol a:** to check the name of the disk in Drive A.

CHAPTER 11

 Copying to and from the Hard Drive

If you don't have a hard drive, go on to Chapter 12.

The primary purpose of making a backup of the hard drive is for security-- so that a copy of the information will exist in the event of some sort of catastrophic hard disk failure. Making backups is one of the most important things you will do with your computer. In the normal course of operation you'll be provided with all kinds of opportunities to make mistakes (like tripping over the power cord..) and without backups, an awful lot of work can disappear.

There are two operations covered in this chapter: 1. moving information from the hard disk to a floppy, which requires the **backup** command, and 2. moving information from a floppy to the hard disk. This second procedure requires the **restore** command.

MAKING BACKUPS WITH THE TANDY 1000

The **backup** and **restore** commands need to be copied onto the hard drive from the Hard Disk Utilities diskette. Place the Hard Disk Utilities diskette in Drive A and type:

copy a:backup.exe c: [ENTER]

Then type:

copy a:restore.exe c: [ENTER]

Copying Files* *from* the Hard Disk

Place a formatted disk in Drive A and at the `C>` prompt type:

backup c: a: [ENTER]

The computer displays the warning:

```
Warning:  All Files will be Deleted on Destination Diskette
Please Insert Backup Diskette into Drive A:
Strike Any Key to CONTINUE
```

MS-DOS is providing the opportunity to change your mind before it starts the backup procedure. It is warning that any files that may already be on Drive A's disk will be erased during the backup.

You already have a formatted disk in Drive A so press the space bar to start the backup.

The screen lists each file's name as it is being copied from Drive C to Drive A. After all files are copied over to the floppy disk, the computer reports:

```
Total number of File(s) Backed Up          32
```

Backing Up One File

Should you want the floppy backup disk to contain only one of the files currently on the hard drive, specify the file's name after the **backup** command. For example, type:

backup c:print.com a: [ENTER]

The warning message is displayed again, indicating that even a single file will

---

* A file is the working unit of information storage. They were compared to "books on a bookshelf" in Chapter 2. All the chapters in Part Three of this book are concerned with files, so you'll become well acquainted with them.

cause all existing files on the floppy to be erased. The screen displays the file name PRINT.COM and indicates:

```
Total number of File(s) Backed Up                    1
```

Check the directory of Drive A. Remember that "whole bunch of files" that used to be on Drive A? All that remains on it is the file we asked for (PRINT.COM) and the file BACKUPID.@@@. (The computer generated this last file as part of the backup procedure.)

Adding a File to the Backup Disk

It is possible to add individual files to the backup floppy without erasing everything on it. This time let's backup the file SORT.EXE without losing the PRINT.COM file. Type:

backup c:sort.exe a:/a ENTER

Check the Drive A directory again. By adding the /a at the end of the **backup** command MS-DOS copied SORT.EXE from the default Drive (C) to Drive A and added it to what was already on that disk.

Backing Up by Date

Whenever a file is created or modified, a date shows up on the directory. (That's what all those dates in the directory are.) A handy backup feature is the ability to back up only those files dated on or after a certain date. Suppose, for example, you wanted to backup all files that were created or modified on Drive C on or after January 1, 1984. Type:

backup c: a:/d:01/01/84 ENTER

...and press the space bar after the warning message. When the backup is complete check the directory of Drive A. Notice that the date for each file is later than 1-01-84.

Another variation of the command is used to backup only those files that have been *modified* since the last backup. Type:

backup c: a:/m [ENTER]

We haven't modified any files at this point so the computer is unable to find a file to backup.

Copying Files *to* the Hard Drive

If you ever really *need* your backed-up data (because you zapped something on the hard drive), you'll need to restore it from the floppy back on to the hard drive. With the disk containing the backed up files in Drive A, type:

restore a: c: [ENTER]

Then press the space bar.

The computer reports the date on which the files were backed up and the diskette number that is being restored. If it took more than one diskette to backup Drive C, the computer keeps track of which disk it is restoring.

If you want to check each file before it is restored, you can use this form of the command:

restore a: c:/p

By adding the **/p** option, you've asked MS-DOS to prompt you before restoring each file.

MAKING BACKUPS WITH THE TANDY 2000

Copying Files* *from* the Hard Drive

Place a formatted disk in Drive A and at the `C>` prompt type:

backup c: a: [ENTER]

The computer displays the warning:

```
Warning:  All Files will be Deleted on Destination Diskette
Please Insert Backup Diskette into Drive A:
Strike Any Key to CONTINUE
```

MS-DOS is providing the opportunity to change your mind before it starts the backup procedure. It is warning that any files that may already be on Drive A's disk will be erased during the backup.

You already have a formatted disk in Drive A so press the space bar to start the backup.

The screen lists each file's name as it is being copied from Drive C to Drive A. After all files are copied over to the floppy disk, the computer reports:

```
Total number of File(s) Backed Up?          32
```

Backing Up One File

Should you want the floppy backup disk to contain only one of the files currently on the hard drive, specify the file's name after the **backup** command. For example, type:

backup c:print.com a: [ENTER]

---

* Files are the working unit of information storage. They were compared to "books on a bookshelf" in Chapter 2. All the chapters in Part Three of this book are concerned with files, so you'll become well acquainted with them.

The warning message is displayed again, indicating that even a single file will cause all existing files on the floppy to be erased. The screen displays the file name PRINT.COM and indicates:

```
Total number of File(s) Backed Up          1
```

Check the directory of Drive A. Remember that "whole bunch of files" that used to be on Drive A? All that remains on it is the file we asked for (PRINT.COM) and the file BACKUPID.@@@. (The computer generated this last file as part of the backup procedure.)

Backing Up by Date

Whenever a file is created or modified, a date shows up on the directory. (That's what all those dates in the directory are.) A handy backup feature is the ability to back up only those files dated on or after a certain date. Suppose, for example, you wanted to backup all files that were created or modified on Drive C on or after January 1, 1984. Type:

backup c: a:/d:01/01/84 `ENTER`

...and press `ENTER` after the warning message. When the backup is complete, check the directory of Drive A. Notice that the date for each file is later than 1-01-84.

Another variation of the command is used to backup only those files that have been *modified* since the last backup. Type:

backup c: a:/m `ENTER`

We haven't modified any files at this point so the computer is unable to find a file to backup.

Copying Files *to* the Hard Drive

If you ever really *need* your backed-up *data* (because you zapped something on the hard drive), you'll need to restore it from the floppy back on to the hard drive. With the disk containing the backed up files in Drive A, type:

restore a: c: $\boxed{\text{ENTER}}$

Then press the space bar.

The computer reports the date on which the files were backed up and the diskette number that is being restored. If it took more than one diskette to backup Drive C, the computer keeps track of which disk it is restoring.

MAKING BACKUPS WITH THE TANDY 1200 HD

The Tandy 1200 HD will not backup files onto a diskette that already contains data. If you attempt to do so, the message:

```
Backup diskette is not blank, Use only formatted,
blank diskettes
```

will appear.

Since we will be trying two backup options in addition to doing a complete backup of the hard drive, you'll need three formatted, blank diskettes. This will prevent having to reformat your one diskette before each option.

Copying Files* *from* the Hard Drive

Place a formatted disk in Drive A and at the C> prompt type:

backup c:*.*a: $\boxed{\text{ENTER}}$

The computer instructs you to:

```
Insert diskette 01 into drive a:
then press enter
```

---

* Files are the working unit of information storage. They were compared to "books on a bookshelf" in Chapter 2. All the chapters in Part Three of this book are concerned with files, so you'll become well acquainted with them.

You already have a formatted disk in Drive A so press ENTER to start the backup.

The screen lists each file's name as it is being copied from Drive C to Drive A. After all files are copied over to the floppy disk, the computer reports:

Backup completed

Backing Up One File

Should you want the floppy backup disk to contain only one of the files currently on the hard drive, specify the file's name after the **backup** command.

Place a new formatted, blank diskette in Drive A, and type:

backup c:\print.com a: ENTER

Press ENTER. The screen displays the file name PRINT.COM and indicates:

Backup completed

Check the directory of Drive A. Remember that "whole bunch of files" on the first backed up diskette? This one has the file we asked for (PRINT.COM) and a couple of additional files generated by the backup procedure.

Backing Up by Date

Whenever a file is created or modified, a date shows up on the directory. (That's what all those dates on the directory are.) A handy backup feature is the ability to back up only those files dated on or after a certain date. Suppose, for example, you wanted to backup all files that were created or modified on Drive C on or after January 1, 1984. Replace the diskette in Drive A with another formatted, blank diskette, and type:

backup c:*.* a: /d(01-01-84) ENTER

Press ENTER again after the insert-diskette instruction. When the backup is complete, check the directory of Drive A. Notice that the date for each file is later than 1-01-84.

Copying Files *to* the Hard Drive

If you ever really *need* your backed-up *data* (because you zapped something on the hard drive), you'll need to restore it from the floppy back on to the hard drive. Insert the disk containing all the backed up files in Drive A, type:

restore a:*.* c: [ENTER]

When the insert-diskette message appears, press [ENTER] as instructed.

The computer reports the date on which the files were backed up and displays the file names as they are restored. If it took more than one diskette to backup Drive C, the computer keeps track of which disk it is restoring. When done, the message:

```
Restore completed
```

is displayed.

SUMMARY

* The **backup** command is used to copy data from the hard drive to a floppy.
* The **restore** command is used to move backed-up data from a floppy to the hard drive.

MAKING BACKUPS OF THE TANDY 1000 HARD DRIVE

1. Insert the Hard Disk Utilities diskette in Drive A.
2. Type **copy a:backup.exe c:** [ENTER] to copy the backup command onto the hard drive.
3. Type **copy a:restore.exe c:** [ENTER] to copy the restore command onto the hard drive.
4. Replace the Hard Disk Utilities disk with a formatted, blank diskette.
5. To copy all the files from the hard disk to a floppy, type **backup c: a:** [ENTER] at the C> prompt.
6. After the warning display comes up, press the space bar.

* To copy one file (named FILENAME) from the Hard Drive to a floppy, type **backup c:filename a:** [ENTER] at the C⟩ prompt.
* To add a file (named FILENAME) to the floppy backup disk, type **backup c:filename a:/a** [ENTER] at the C⟩ prompt.
* To backup by date, type **backup c: a:/d:mm/dd/yy** [ENTER] at the C⟩ prompt. (*mm* = month, *dd* = day, *yy* = year)
* To backup only modified files, type **backup c: a:/m** [ENTER].

To copy files from the floppy backup disk to the hard drive:
1. Insert diskette with backup in Drive A.
2. Type **restore a: c:** [ENTER].
3. Press the space bar.

* To check a file before restoring it, type **restore a: c:/p** [ENTER].

MAKING BACKUPS OF THE TANDY 2000 HARD DRIVE
1. Insert a formatted floppy disk in Drive A.
2. At the C⟩ prompt, type **backup c: a:** [ENTER].
3. After the warning is displayed, press the space bar.

* To copy one file (named FILENAME) from the hard drive to a floppy, type **backup c:filename a:** [ENTER] at the C⟩ prompt.
* To backup by date, type **backup c: a:/d:mm/dd/yy** [ENTER] at the C⟩ prompt. (*mm* = month, *dd* = day, *yy* = year)
* To backup only modified files, type **backup c: a:/m** [ENTER].

To copy files from the floppy backup disk to the hard drive:
1. Insert diskette with backup in Drive A.
2. Type **restore a: c:** [ENTER].
3. Press the space bar.

MAKING BACKUPS OF THE TANDY 1200 HD
* A *blank*, formatted diskette must be used each time a backup--whether of one or all files--is made.

1. Insert a formatted, blank diskette in Drive A.
2. At the C⟩ prompt, type **backup c:*.*a:** [ENTER].
3. Press [ENTER].

* To copy one file (named FILENAME) from the hard drive to a floppy, type **backup c:filename a:** [ENTER].
* To backup by date, type **backup c:*.* a: /d(mm-dd-yy)** [ENTER]. (*mm* = month, *dd* = day, *yy* = year)

To copy files from the floppy backup disk to the hard drive:
1. Insert diskette with backup in Drive A.
2. Type **restore a:*.* c:** [ENTER].
3. Press [ENTER] again.

CHAPTER 12

Comparing Two Diskettes

Comparing Two Diskettes (floppy only)

Backup copies of diskettes are a way of life with computers. We've already suggested you use a copy of the MS-DOS diskette for everyday use, and when you begin saving your own data "on-disk," the practice of keeping backup copies will save you a lot of grief due to lost or damaged diskettes. One of the drawbacks of having copies, however, is that it can get confusing if you forget which was the latest copy. Was a copy made after the last minor change? Is this an exact copy, or has someone made some changes you're not aware of?

The only certain way is to compare the two disks in question, a byte at a time. There is a command to do this for the 1000/1200 HD, and another command for the 2000. Read the section below that applies to your computer.

TANDY 1000 AND 1200 HD

Put your original MS-DOS disk back in Drive A and the copy of it in Drive B and type:

diskcomp a: b: [ENTER]

One-Drive System
Simply type **diskcomp** [ENTER]. As usual, you will be prompted when it's time to swap disks.

MS-DOS asks you to insert the disks you want compared:

```
Insert first diskette in drive A:
Strike any key when ready
```

You've done that, so tap the space bar and you're asked to:

```
Insert second diskette in drive B:
Strike any key when ready
```

...which you've also done. Tap the space bar again.

Press any key. MS-DOS gears up for the comparison, and delivers the following message:

```
Comparing 9 sectors per track, 2 side(s)*
```

When the comparison is finished, MS-DOS reports that:

```
Diskettes compare ok
```

...and offers to:

```
Compare more diskettes (Y/N)?
```

Press Y and when prompted to do so, insert the formatted disk you named SAMPLE_DISK into Drive A. Put a blank, unnamed formatted disk in Drive

---

* Every computer covered by this book uses "9-sector" tracks. All that means is that the concentric rings, or tracks, laid down on the diskette during formatting are further divided into individual segments called sectors. It helps the computer find things, but it's nothing that you, the operator, should ever have to worry about. Older versions of MS-DOS used 8-sector tracks, so, should you ever find yourself comparing two of these older disks, the command to use would be **diskcomp/8**. Older versions also used single-sided diskettes, and to compare two of those, the command is **diskcomp/1**. To do both, use **diskcomp/8/1**.

B (or prepare to swap them back and forth in Drive A if you have a single drive). The two disks you'll be comparing this time should be identical with the exception of the name, or "Volume Label". Type the command **diskcomp a: b:** (skip the **a: b:** if you have only one drive), and let's see what happens.

A few seconds into the job a new message appears:

```
Compare error(s) on
Track 0, Side 0

Compare error(s) on
Track 0, Side 1
```

This sounds like MS-DOS is telling us to do something, but it's not. It's just saying it found a "compare error" on Track 0, Side 0, and another one on Track 0, Side 1. Computer engineers like to use "0" for the first item on a list. The 9 tracks on a disk are numbered 0 through 8, and the two sides are 0 and 1.

Looks like the name, SAMPLE_DISK, is recorded on the first track on each side of the disk. Any compare errors found by MS-DOS indicate that the disks are not identical, and that's the purpose of the **diskcomp** command.

TANDY 2000

The 2000 provides a couple of extra features. In addition to simply comparing two disks, it will make a copy of a disk and then compare it to the original. It will also format a new disk, use it to make a copy of the original, then compare the two.

We'll be using the MS-DOS diskette as a sample "source" disk in this chapter, but you can replace it with any disk you'd like to compare or duplicate when prompted on the screen to do so.

To make a simple comparison on the 2000, place the original MS-DOS diskette in Drive A and the copy of it in Drive B and type:

compdupe [ENTER]

A copyright notice appears on the screen, along with some information about different *kinds* of compdupes (which we'll come back to shortly) and the instruction to press the space bar when ready. This is also when the prompt instructing you to insert source and destination disks appears, in the event you don't want to use the one(s) currently in the drive(s). When you're ready, press the space bar.

The computer displays a line of dashes to represent each track on the disks. As each track passes the comparison test, the dash is changed to a dot.

Watch the dash closely as the comparison is being made. Notice that an asterisk (*) appears before the dash is replaced with a dot. The asterisk means that the computer compared the data on that track and found no errors. The asterisk is one of several symbols used to report the status of the comparison. Had the computer found a difference between the two disks, the dash would be replaced with the letter C.

When the comparison is finished, MS-DOS asks:

AGAIN (Y/N):

Press [Y] and when prompted to do so, insert the formatted disk you named SAMPLE_DISK into Drive A. Put a blank, unnamed formatted disk in Drive B (or prepare to swap them back and forth in Drive A if you have a single drive). The two disks you'll be comparing this time should be identical with the exception of the name, or "Volume Label". Press the space bar and watch the screen.

Notice that the first dash is changed to an asterisk followed by the letter C. As soon as the first difference is encountered, MS-DOS stops the comparison and announces:

Disks do not compare

AGAIN (Y/N):

Answer by pressing [N]

Looks like the name, SAMPLE_DISK, is recorded on the very first track of the disk. Any comparison errors found by MS-DOS indicate that the disks are not identical, and that's the purpose of the **compdupe** command.

Duplicating Disks

In Chapter 7 you learned how to format a disk and later you used a formatted disk to make a copy of the master diskette. With the **compdupe** command we have the options of formatting, duplicating and comparing two diskettes all in one step by typing a slight variation of the **compdupe** command. (This is the first of those "different kinds of compdupes" we said we'd come back to.)

Place the MS-DOS disk in Drive A and a blank *unformatted* disk in Drive B and type:

compdupe /d [ENTER]

When the message appears, press the space bar. This time the computer reads the data on Drive A and reports a successful read by displaying an asterisk. It then formats that track on the disk in Drive B, copies the data onto it and compares what it copied with the original. If no errors occurred, the asterisk is replaced with a dot and the computer moves on to the next track.

If the computer has a problem formatting one of the tracks in the new disk the dash for that track will be replaced with the letter F. Another possible error can occur when the computer is unable to write the data to the formatted track. Should this occur, the dash is replaced with the letter D. If an error does occur with the new diskette during the duplicating process, bulk erase the diskette (with a magnetic bulk eraser, available at most Radio Shack stores), and try again, or start over with another new disk.

Once the entire disk is copied without errors, the computer reports:

```
Disks duplicated with no errors

AGAIN (Y/N):
```

Duplicating Formatted Disks

When you already have formatted blank disks available, the format step can be skipped in the **compdupe**. Leave the MS-DOS disk in Drive A, and insert a blank *formatted* diskette in Drive B. (Single-drive users have a blank formatted disk ready for swapping with the MS-DOS disk when prompted to do so.)

Answer the AGAIN (Y/N) question with an [N] then type:

compdupe /d /s [ENTER]

The /d tells the computer to duplicate the disk before comparing and the /s tells it to skip the format routine.

By skipping the format routine the duplication procedure takes a little less time than it did before--it takes time to format each track.

SUMMARY

TANDY 1000 AND 1200 HD
* Type **diskcomp a: b:** to compare two diskettes (**diskcomp** for single-drive systems).
* If differences are found, MS-DOS reports Compare error(s).
* Sides of a diskette are called 0 and 1
* The 9 tracks on a diskette are numbered 0-8

TANDY 2000
* Type **compdupe** to compare two disks.
* Type **compdupe** /d to format, duplicate and compare two disks.
* Type **compdupe** /d /s to duplicate (skip formatting) and compare two disks.

CHAPTER 13

Checking the Disk

Another Way to Look at a Disk

As you know, the **dir** command produces a list of all the files on a particular disk, along with some other useful information. The **chkdsk** (check disk) command provides a quick rundown of the memory situation--what the space on the disk is being used for, how many bytes are available, and how much of the computer's own RAM memory is currently being used. In multiple-drive systems, the disk in any drive can be checked. Just specify the drive after giving the command. With the MS-DOS disk in Drive A, type:

chkdsk a: `ENTER`*

MS-DOS responds with a short report:

```
362496 bytes total disk space
 23552 bytes in 2 hidden files
278528 bytes in 29 user files
 60416 bytes available on disk

245760 bytes total memory
220608 bytes free
```

---

* This also works with the hard disk; just use **chkdsk c:** `ENTER`

Your numbers may vary, of course, depending upon the computer you are using. This is a handy little report, one that you should run from time to time when you think you might be getting low on memory or disk space. The "hidden files" referred to are MS-DOS's own *system* files--those that actually control MS-DOS. Since they don't show up on the directory, they're called hidden files. (In case you're curious, the names of the hidden files are IO.SYS and MSDOS.SYS.)

The "user files" listed are the other programs that come with MS-DOS--the ones accessed by the so-called "external" commands, like **format** and **diskcopy**. If you were to save any of your own files on this disk, they would be included under user files.

The "total memory" number refers to the computer's RAM. If your machine advertises 256K, you actually have 245760 bytes total RAM available. Because of the amount of RAM currently being used by MS-DOS, the computer (in the above example) can spare you a little over 220 kilobytes for your own work before you have to transfer some of it onto a disk and "clean house" to make room for more.

The **chkdsk** command can also perform a couple of other tricks. In the event any errors are encountered during the check, they will be flagged, or in some cases, can be corrected. Since the MS-DOS disk (hopefully) has no errors resulting from improper saving, we won't be able to demonstrate it now, but the command to fix errors is **chkdsk/f**. Before the short report (above) appears, any necessary error messages will be displayed, and any errors MS-DOS can fix will be automatically taken care of. Remember this for later when something doesn't seem to be acting right--there may be an error in one of your files that **chkdsk/f** can fix.

An even more detailed check can be made with a variation of the command. **chkdsk/v** not only checks and repairs, it provides detailed messages about any errors it finds.

There is one other variation of **chkdsk**. We haven't talked much about files yet, but you have seen the names of all the ones on the MS-DOS disk, and you know what they are--the major unit in which information is stored on the disk; the "book" on the bookshelf represented by the disk.

If a file is big enough to require more than one segment to hold it, MS-DOS normally breaks it into adjacent segments. As files are added, they are lined up along the tracks, neat as you please. But when a file you no longer need is deleted, the remaining files don't move up. The deleted file just leaves a hole. Eventually, you could end up with files scattered all over the surface of the disk, with vacant spots in between.

MS-DOS, however, doesn't believe in wasting space so when asked to save a long file, it's likely to distribute pieces of it among several of these small vacancies. This disjointing of a file into non-contiguous areas of the disk has no effect on you or your work, except that the computer may take a little longer to load a file into RAM since it has to go on a scavenger hunt for the pieces.

If you like things tidy and you're concerned about a very important file being chopped up into too many parts (or if it seems to be taking a long time to load), you can check to see if the file is contiguous by using the **chkdsk** command. Add to the command the full name of the file in question. Let's pick one from the MS-DOS directory--say, PRINT.COM (the period separates the file name from its extension--we'll get into all that later). Type the command and the file name:

chkdsk print.com [ENTER]

The same report appears, followed by the message:

```
All specified file(s) are contiguous,
```

Should the file in which you're interested be fragmented, MS-DOS will say so, and you can move it to a fresh disk where there is room to keep it all together. (We'll move a file from one disk to another in Chapter 17.)

SUMMARY

* Type **chkdsk a:** to check the disk in Drive A.
* To check for and repair errors on Drive A, type **chkdsk/f a:**.
* To check, repair and obtain detailed error messages, type **chkdsk/v a:**.
* When files are deleted, new files are broken up and stored in the vacant spaces. Type **chkdsk** and the file name to determine if a file is contiguous.

CHAPTER 14

Review of Part Two

Part Two has been an introduction to the MS-DOS commands that are used to prepare and handle your diskettes. A Tandy 1000 or 1200 HD floppy disk can store approximately 120 pages of text. Tandy 2000 disks hold approximately 240 pages. The 10 megabyte hard drive holds about 3000 pages, 15 meg. holds 4500 and so on.

If your computer has 128K of built-in (RAM) memory, you can have up to approximately 38 pages loaded and active at any one time. Double that number for 256K and so on.

Each disk must be *formatted* before it can be used to store information, and copies or *backups* of all important disks should be kept for security.

Both floppy and hard drive disks need to be protected from accidental erasures or changes. While all floppies can be protected with write protect tabs, only some external hard drives have write protect switches.

On the Tandy 1200 HD, a *blank,* formatted diskette must be used each time a backup is made.

COMMANDS

format b: formats the diskette in Drive B. Other drives may be specified.

format/v b: provides opportunity to name diskette in Drive B.

copy a:*.* c: (Tandy 1000/1200 HD only) copies the MS-DOS files to the hard disk.

diskcopy a: b: copies the disk in Drive A to a blank, formatted disk in Drive B.

vol a: displays the name of the diskette in Drive A.

backup c: a: (Tandy 1000/2000 only) copies files from the hard drive (Drive C) to Drive A.

backup c:somefile a: (Tandy 1000/2000 only) copies only the file named SOMEFILE from Drive C to Drive A. Any other files already on Drive A will be erased.

backup c: a:/d:01/01/84 (Tandy 1000/2000 only) copies all files dated Jan. 1, 1984 or later from Drive C to Drive A.

backup c: a:/m (Tandy 1000/2000 only) copies only those files that have been modified since the last backup from Drive C to A.

restore a: c: (Tandy 1000/2000 only) copies all files from Drive A to Drive C. Hard disk is not erased, but any files on the hard disk with the same name as on the floppy will be written over.

diskcomp a: b: (Tandy 1000/1200 HD only) compares the disk in Drive A to the one in Drive B.

chkdsk a: checks the disk in Drive a for errors.

chkdsk/f a: checks the disk in Drive A and repairs some errors.

chkdsk/v a: checks the disk in Drive A, repairs errors and displays error messages.

chkdsk followed by a file name determines if the file is continguous or distributed over disk in spaces left by cancelled files.

TANDY 1000 ONLY

hsect begins formatting the hard drive.

fdisk begins initialization of the hard drive.

hformat c: /b/s/v prepares the hard disk to receive MS-DOS.

copy a:backup.exe c: copies the **backup** command from the Hard Disk Utilities disk to the hard drive.

copy a:restore.exe c: copies the **restore** command from the Hard Disk Utilities disk to the hard drive.

backup c:somefile a:/a copies only the file named SOMEFILE from Drive C and *adds* it to Drive A. Does not erase other files from Drive A.

restore a: c:/p prompts the user to decide which files are to be copied from Drive A to Drive C.

TANDY 2000 ONLY

confighd begins formatting the hard drive.

compdupe compares the disk in Drive A to the one in Drive B.

compdupe /d formats the disk in Drive B, uses it to make a copy of the disk in Drive A, then compres the two.

compdupe /d /s copies the disk in Drive A onto the disk in Drive B, but skips the formatting step. A formatted disk must be inserted in Drive B. If the disk in Drive B contains data, it will be written over.

TANDY 1200 HD ONLY

---

llfdfmt begins formatting the hard drive.

part displays the Partition Menu and begins phase two of the format procedure.

format c: /s/f prepares the hard disk to recieve MS-DOS.

backup c:*.* a: copies all files from the hard drive (Drive C) to Drive A.

backup c:\somefile a: copies only the file named SOMEFILE from Drive C to Drive A.

backup c:*.* a: /d(01-01-84) copies all files dated Jan. 1, 1984 or later from Drive C to Drive A.

restore a:*.* c: copies all files from Drive A to Drive C.

PART 3

Using MS-DOS to manage your files

CHAPTER 15

What's a File?

What's a File?

We've suggested a couple of times that a file on a disk could be considered roughly equivalent to a book on a bookshelf. Or if you like, think of it as a file in a filing cabinet. In any case, it is the basic unit of storage for computer data. Just as there are books for different purposes--books for reading, books for reference and so on--there are also disk files for different purposes. We could go into great detail about the subtle differences among file types, but for now, all you need to know are the three primary types of files: *program files*, *data files* and *system files*.

Program Files

Program files usually make the computer do something; for instance, the FORMAT file on the MS-DOS disk contains the instructions to the computer which cause it to format a disk. The program is started with the command **format**. Most of the files on the MS-DOS disk are programs, and their extensions are either .COM for command or .EXE for executable. All the commands we refer to as "external" commands trigger program files. If you add some application programs, such as a word processor or a spreadsheet to your system, these will be made up of program files.

Data Files

Data files are the kind you fill with your own data--letters written using the word processor, budgets and forecasts using the spreadsheet and so on. Data files are generally given the extensions .DAT (data) or .TXT (text). *Generally speaking*, data files are in language readable by you, and program files are in language the machine can read ("machine language").

System Files

Files with the extension .SYS are the heart of MS-DOS. These files contain the information MS-DOS needs to communicate with the computer. While .COM and .EXE *program files* such as FORMAT.COM and DISK-COPY.COM could be considered external "accessories" to MS-DOS, the *system files* are the "engine" and "transmission" that make the whole thing go. In addition to all their behind-the-scenes work, the system files also contain the internal commands, like **dir** and **copy**. It is because the system files remain in memory at all times that these internal commands work immediately, without the necessity of going to the disk. Even if you remove the MS-DOS disk, once MS-DOS has been loaded, the system files are still there in memory to keep things running.

Although the above covers the file types you will most commonly use, there are a few others you should be aware of.

Batch Files

The number of commands available make MS-DOS a very powerful system. It is possible to make it even more powerful, however, by chaining a "batch" of commands together, saving the whole series in a special file and accessing it with a single command. As you learn more commands, you'll probably begin to see some interesting possibilities for this trick, and in Volume 2, we'll go into batch file building in detail.

BASIC Files

One of the programs that comes with MS-DOS is BASIC. BASIC, in case you aren't really sure, is a "language," a program designed to allow you to create your own programs. Programs you create using BASIC will have the extension .BAS. We'll do a little program writing in the next chapter.

PROGRAM FILES

Programs, such as FORMAT.COM and DISKCOPY.COM., that cause the computer to perform useful tasks. Usually written in machine language and loaded by single-word commands: (**format**, **diskcopy**). Extensions: .COM, .EXE.

DATA FILES

Information or text created by user. Usually written in plain English. Examples: documents created using word processors or lists of figures created using spreadsheet programs. Extensions: .TXT, .DAT

SYSTEM FILES

The built-in parts of MS-DOS. Control such things as screen layouts, keyboard functions and general file-handling procedures. Also operate "internal" commands, such as **dir** and **cls**. Extension: .SYS.

OTHERS

1. Batch files: Sequences of commands stored in a file, designed to execute a complex chain of events at a single command. Extension: .BAT

2. BASIC files: User-created programs written and executed using the BASIC programming language. Extension: .BAS.

CHAPTER 16

Creating a Sample File Using BASIC

BASIC Programming Language

One of the "accessory" programs that comes with MS-DOS is the BASIC programming language. BASIC is a subject about which entire books have been written. We're going to give you just a taste of it here because it's a handy tool for creating some sample files to put on one of your formatted data diskettes. Once you have some files to work with, we can demonstrate more of MS-DOS's capabilities.

BASIC programming, by the way, can be very useful and a lot of fun. If you are interested in learning it, we recommend, as a start-to-finish tutorial course, **Learning BASIC for the Tandy 1000/2000** (Radio Shack Cat. No. 25-1500). As a reference book, there is no substitute for **The BASIC Handbook** (available at bookstores). Both are by David A. Lien and published by CompuSoft Publishing.

Loading BASIC

BASIC itself is a program file, and it can be accessed by simply typing its name. With the MS-DOS disk in Drive A, a formatted diskette in Drive B and the system prompt on the screen, type:

basic [ENTER]

One-Drive Systems
After typing **basic**, remove the MS-DOS disk and insert a blank formatted diskette.

Tandy 2000
Users with the High-Resolution Graphics option will see a blank screen and the keyboard will appear "frozen" after entering BASIC. If this is your case, press the Reset switch and watch the light on the NUM LOCK or CAPS key. The light will go out as soon as Reset is pressed. After a couple seconds, the light will flash on and off. When this happens, immediately tap the F12 key. The computer is fussy about when F12 must be pressed, so keep trying until you are successful then type:

basic ENTER

MS-DOS gives you a clue that you've just loaded a major program by presenting a copyright notice. At the top of your screen you should see the name of the program: GW-BASIC (or Model 2000 BASIC), a version number and some copyright and licensing information. Under that, there is a memory amount similar to this:

60875 Bytes free (Your number may vary, depending on your equipment.)

BASIC allows you to use only a fixed block of memory--in this example, about 60k--even though your computer may be equipped with more RAM. Advanced users can get to some more memory, but for our purposes, what BASIC gives you is enough.

Under the memory notice is BASIC's own "system prompt":

Ok

This prompt has the same function as the MS-DOS system prompt. It means the program is not busy--it's Ok for you to go ahead and do something. The Ok prompt also serves to remind you that you are in BASIC.

At the bottom of the screen there is a row of numbers, each followed by a word. The first is LIST, the second is RUN and so on. These represent the *function keys*, the keys on the keyboard labeled [F1] through [F12] (through [F10] on the 1200 HD). Only ten of the twelve keys are being used. The function keys are nothing more than shortcut keys; they do in one keystroke what would take three or four to do "manually." We'll only be using a couple of them for our purposes. You'll see how they work in just a moment.

Because BASIC is a language, or a "programmer's program," we can use it to create programs of our own. Those you create in this chapter will give you a small taste of what a BASIC program can do, and they will give you some sample files to play with. This chapter will not be a lesson in BASIC; we'll simply walk you through a few short programs.

Line Numbers

Every line in a BASIC program tells the computer, in a language it understands, to do something. Therefore, each line must be a distinctly numbered instruction. It is customary to number BASIC lines by tens--10, 20, 30 etc.

Sample Program 1 - Math Calculation

Math is one of the things a computer does best, so our first program will do a little math problem. We'll give the computer a few numbers, then ask it to add and subtract them. BASIC will accept either upper- or lowercase, but when you're finished typing, it converts everything (except whatever is enclosed in quotes) to uppercase. Just to make things simpler, press the [CAPS] key and, type the programs in uppercase.

At the Ok prompt, type your first numbered line:

10 REM MATH CALCULATION

REM in BASIC means *remark*. A REM line does not cause the computer to do anything. It's just there to provide information to you. You can stick a REM line anywhere in a program. Finish typing in the following program, pressing [ENTER] at the end of each line:

20 A = 1000
30 B = 750
40 C = 25
50 PRINT A-B + C

When a computer is running a BASIC program, it starts at the first line and works its way down through each successive line. When this little program is run, it will ignore the first line, the REM line, then observe that A = 1000, that B = 750 and that C = 25. These are just arbitrary values we chose for the real work which is in line 50. Line 50 tells the computer to print (on the screen) the sum of 1000-750 + 25.

All it takes to run a BASIC program is typing the word **RUN** [ENTER], but notice that there is a function key that even does that for you. Press the [F2] key. [F2] automatically "types" **RUN** [ENTER], and almost immediately, the answer to the math problem appears.

```
RUN
  275
Ok
```

You've just written and run a computer program. You put in some numbers, and the computer calculated them and gave you the answer asked for in your program. In a very simple way, this program demonstrates what every computer program does; it gives the computer instructions. The computer goes through them, one at a time, and performs the tasks as instructed. Play with the program a little. Change line 40 to C = 50. All that's required to change a BASIC program line is to type that line over--no need to type the whole program over*. Type:

40 C = 50 [ENTER]

...and press [F2] to run it again. Predictably, a change in the problem causes a change in the answer, which is now 300.

---

*If you already know something about BASIC, you probably know that there are ways to edit program lines without typing the whole line over. This way is simple and good enough for our purposes.

To see your program in its new form, it is necessary to *list* it, and if you'll refer to the bottom of the screen, you'll see that function key [F1] accomplishes this task. Press [F1] [ENTER].

There's the program again, with a new line 40. Change any of the lines, including the equation in line 50. The sign for "divided by" in BASIC is the /, and for "multiplied by", use *. You can even use parentheses, just like you do on paper. Whatever numbers you use in whatever equation you create, BASIC will give you an answer when you press [F2] to run.

When you're finished experimenting with this sample program, *save* it onto the formatted data disk by pressing the **SAVE"** function key [F4] and typing the designator of the drive holding your formatted data diskette, which is B: in a two-drive system or A: in a one-drive system (C: for the hard drive):

SAVE"B:MATH" [ENTER]

The " separating the command SAVE from the name is required by BASIC, so the function key puts it in automatically. The " after the name is good programming practice, so be sure to type it in.

Notice that when you assign a certain drive to a file name, the drive designation goes *before* the name. This rule applies to all MS-DOS files, not just BASIC files.

The disk spins when you press [ENTER], and your first file is saved on the new disk. Before we leave BASIC to look at the directory (and while we're on a roll...), let's add a couple more.

Clearing the Memory

One thing about BASIC, it believes everything it sees. If you have one program loaded (like MATH) and you type in another program, BASIC will try to run them both and get confused. Whenever you're finished working with one BASIC program, make sure it's been saved to the disk, then type:

NEW [ENTER]

This clears out whatever is in memory so that any new program won't conflict with the old. Now type this second sample program (remember to [ENTER] at the end of each line):

Sample Program 2 - Greeting

10 REM GREETING
20 INPUT "WHAT IS YOUR NAME";A$
30 PRINT "HELLO THERE, ";A$

Don't worry too much about how the program works, just try to type it accurately. Watch those quotation marks (") and semi-colons (;) and the comma and space after HELLO THERE.

Press [F2] to run the program, and when asked your name, type it in and press [ENTER]. Once the computer has said hello to you and returned the Ok prompt, save it as B:GREETING with the [F4] key.

You now have a program that does a math problem and one that talks to you; how about one more that does a useful job? Once GREETING is saved, type **NEW** to clear the memory and **CLS** (remember **CLS**?) to clear the clutter off the screen, then type this program:

Sample Program 3 - Celsius to Fahrenheit Conversion

10 REM CELSIUS TO FAHRENHEIT CONVERSION
20 INPUT "WHAT IS THE TEMPERATURE IN DEGREES (C)";C
30 F = (9/5)*C + 32
40 PRINT C;"DEGREES (C) = ";F;"DEGREES (F)."
50 PRINT : GOTO 20

When you run this little gem, it will ask you for a Celsius temperature. Type any number and [ENTER]. The Fahrenheit equivalent of the temperature you typed will instantly appear, and you'll be asked for the next temperature you'd like converted. To stop the cycle and get back to the Ok prompt, press the [BREAK] key ([Ctrl] [Break] on the 1200 HD) at the upper right of the keyboard. Save the program as B:CONVERT.

Loading a BASIC Program from the Disk

There's another function key you may be wondering about--the F3 "Load" key. Yes, it is used for loading BASIC programs. Clear the memory with **NEW** and the screen with **CLS**, then press F3 and type the name of one of your new files; for example:

F3 **B:GREETING** ENTER

All you will see is the OK prompt, but the program is indeed loaded. If you want to see it, press F1 ENTER (to list). To run it, press F2.

Getting Back to MS-DOS

With three sample programs under your belt, it's time to end this brief excursion into BASIC and get back to MS-DOS. To do that, type:

SYSTEM ENTER

One-Drive SYSTEM
You will have to put the MS-DOS disk back in to reload MS-DOS or to use any other "external" command, such as diskcopy or format.

---

* The BASIC programming language is a program that comes with MS-DOS.
* Load BASIC by typing **BASIC** ENTER.
* List a BASIC program by typing **LIST** ENTER or by pressing F1 ENTER.
* Run a BASIC program by typing **RUN** ENTER or by pressing F2.
* Load a BASIC program by typing **LOAD"** or by pressing F3. Then type the name of the file you wish to load and press ENTER.
* Save a BASIC program by typing **SAVE"** or by pressing F4. Then type the name under which you wish to save the file and ENTER. (The name may include the drive designation.)
* To clear RAM memory of the currently loaded BASIC file(s) to prepare for another, type **NEW** ENTER.
* When specifying a certain drive in a file name, the drive designation goes at the beginning of the name. Example: B:MATH.
* To close BASIC and return to MS-DOS, type **SYSTEM** ENTER.

CHAPTER 17

Copying Files

Now that you have some sample files on your data disk, you can begin using some of MS-DOS's file handling features. File handling? Most of your computer work will probably be with an application program--a word processor, a spreadsheet, a database or a programming language, etc. Every application stores information in the form of files, and most have some file handling capabilities of their own. It's often more convenient, however, to use the operating system to copy files or compare them or delete them and so on. When you let MS-DOS do the job, you can work on files from several different applications at the same time, and you can look at the directories, rearrange a few files, then go right back to the directory again to check your work.

Speaking of directories, let's check the data disk to see if those new BASIC program files made it. Be sure the data disk is in Drive B and the system prompt is on the screen, then type **dir b:**

One-Drive Systems
Put the data disk in the drive and type **dir**.

```
 Volume in drive B is SAMPLE DISK
Directory of  B:
```

```
MATH     BAS      68     9-25-85   10:15a
GREETING BAS      57     9-25-85   10:20a
CONVERT  BAS     165     9-25-85   10:30a
          3 File(s)     359424 bytes free

A>
```

There they are--all the new files. BASIC automatically added the BAS extension to them for you, which means that from now on, you'll have to refer to them by their full names, including the **.BAS**. The period does not show up on the directory, but you must include it whenever you type the file name so that MS-DOS will know you intend the extension to be just that, an extension, and not part of the actual name. (The 2000 stores files differently, so the numbers in the size column will not be the same for you.)

For starters, let's try making a copy of MATH.BAS on the same disk.

Making a Copy of a File on the Same Disk

The copy command is just what you'd expect it to be: **copy**. There can't be two files on the same disk with the same name, however, so if you want a duplicate of MATH.BAS on this disk, you'll have to give the copy another name. Type:

copy b:math.bas b:newmath.bas ⌷ENTER⌷

One-Drive Systems
Substitute **a:** for **b:**.

Check the directory again to see NEWMATH.BAS listed. One-drive users notice that the MS-DOS disk doesn't have to be in the drive to use the copy command; it's an internal command, and it stays in memory even when the MS-DOS disk is removed.

Copying a File to a Different Disk

Since the MS-DOS disk is not needed for file copying (once MS-DOS is "booted up"), it's a simple matter to copy files from one disk to another by simply specifying drives. The disk containing your files (which we'll refer to as the *source* disk) is already in Drive B, so put another blank, formatted disk (the *target* disk) in Drive A, and type:

copy b:math.bas a:math.bas ENTER

Notice it's perfectly all right to use the same name if copying to another disk.

To copy a file from Drive A to Drive B, just reverse the drive designations when you give the copy command.

Hard-Drive Systems

All you have to remember is that the hard drive is Drive C. MS-DOS is on it, as well as all your files. To copy from the hard drive to a floppy, put the floppy in Drive A and use the command **copy c:math.bas a:math.bas** ENTER

One-Drive Systems

To copy a file from one disk to another in a single-drive system it's necessary to fool the computer into thinking it has two drives. At the A> prompt, type:

copy a:math.bas b:math.bas ENTER

The computer responds with:

```
Insert diskette for drive B: and
strike any key when ready
```

Remove the data disk from the drive, and insert a second formatted disk. Strike any key. MS-DOS reports that it has copied one file and returns the A> prompt. It still thinks of the diskette as Drive B however, so to see a directory of it, you must type

dir b: ENTER

A simple **dir** command (without the drive designation) causes MS-DOS to ask you to insert the disk for Drive A. Put the original disk back in and strike any key, and you're back to normal.

SUMMARY

* To copy a file to the same disk you must give it a new name.
  Example: **copy b:oldname b:newname**
* To copy a file to a different disk, you may use the same name, but change the drive designation.
  Example: **copy a:oldname b:oldname**
* Files created in BASIC are automatically given the extension .BAS.

CHAPTER 18

Shortcuts and Wildcards

Shortcuts

MS-DOS will *assume* the current drive number. In other words, if you have MATH.BAS in Drive A and you want to copy it, you don't have to specify A:MATH.BAS. The computer will automatically look on Drive A for any file it is asked for. If it doesn't find the file on A, it will say File not found.

To copy MATH.BAS from A to B, type:

copy math.bas b:math.bas [ENTER]

This reads "Copy MATH.BAS (from Drive A, the default drive) to Drive B and call it MATH.BAS over there too."

The command can be further shortened by allowing MS-DOS to assume that the name of the copy will be the same as the name of the original, unless you specify differently. Typing:

copy math.bas b: [ENTER]

...means, "Copy MATH.BAS (from the default drive) to Drive B and give it the same name it had originally."

Changing the Default Drive

Normally, the default drive is Drive A and normally that's where the MS-DOS system disk is kept. That's why the system prompt is A>. If you plan to do a lot with the disk in another drive (B, in a two-drive system, or higher if you have a hard drive), changing the default is simply a matter of typing:

b: [ENTER]

Now the system prompt is B>, and it won't be necessary to specify the **b:** drive designator when you ask for files from the disk in Drive B.

What Happens When MS-DOS Is Not in the Default Drive?

It's convenient to have the default be the drive which holds your data files (in this case, B), but what happens when you type an external MS-DOS command, like **diskcopy**, or **basic**? MS-DOS is now looking at Drive B, but if the MS-DOS disk is in Drive A, those commands are still located down there. Typing an external command alone will result in an error message.

To tell MS-DOS to look for commands on Drive A when some other drive is the default, type:

path a: [ENTER]

The \ is on the [7] key in the numeric keypad.(On the 1200 HD, the \ is located to the left of the *left* [Shift] key.) Be sure the [NUM LOCK] light is not on. Now, you can work in Drive B, but should you give a command that requires Drive A, MS-DOS will be able to find it.

Return to A by typing:

a: [ENTER]

One-Drive SYSTEM
You won't be able to use MS-DOS commands, of course, unless the MS-DOS disk is in the drive.

Wildcards

The * character can be used as a *wildcard* to take the place of a file name or extension. This is normally used to copy a whole group of files, all with the same name or extension. For example:

copy *.bas b: would copy all BASIC files from Drive A to Drive B.

copy sample.* b: would copy all files named SAMPLE, no matter what extension each had, from Drive A to Drive B.

Let's try a couple of things. With the data disk containing your sample BASIC files in Drive B, type:

b: ENTER

...to change the default to Drive B, then:

copy *.bas *.dog ENTER

Each of the BASIC file names appear on the screen as they are being copied. When the ß⟩ prompt returns, pull a directory. There should now be eight files on the disk--the original four with .BAS extensions and the same four again with .DOG extensions. (Remember, in naming your files you can make up extensions as well as names.)

Try it again, this time using the extension .CAT.

copy *.dog *.cat ENTER or **copy *.bas *.cat** ENTER

Now the directory shows twelve files; three sets with three different extensions. This could be useful for duplicating a series of matching "templates" or formats. For example, you might use Multiplan to design a spreadsheet called INCOME.MAY and another one called EXPENSE.MAY, and maybe a few others. Then, back in MS-DOS, copy all *.MAY files to *.JUN, then to *.JUL and so on.

Another approach would be to copy all EXPENSE.* files to some other file name. Try it with our GREETING files. Type:

copy greeting.* howdy.* ENTER

All three GREETINGs are duplicated to new files called HOWDY.

Wildcards with Directories

The wildcard can also be helpful when looking at directories. To see a list of only your BASIC files, type:

dir *.bas [ENTER]

A listing of only those files with the .BAS extension appears. In a large directory, when you're looking for something in particular, this could be very helpful. Try it again using ***.dog** and again with ***.cat**.

Try it when the file name is known, but not the extension:

dir math.* [ENTER]

...or when only part of the file name is known:

dir greet* [ENTER]

This one will be especially handy as your directories grow and will be a big help if you plan for it by beginning associated file names with the same few letters--for example: SALES1, SALES2, SALES3, etc. With a set of related files like those, a request for **dir sales*** will produce a directory of all files beginning with SALES.

Copying an Entire Disk Using the Wildcard

When the default is Drive A (A⟩), **copy *.* b:** copies *all* files from Drive A to Drive B. When the default is B, **copy *.* a:** copies all files from B to A. These things can be switched around; all you have to remember is that files in the default drive don't have to have their drive designations specified.

This is a good way to clean up fragmented files. Remember we discussed files getting broken up to fit vacant sectors in the disk? A straight diskcopy will copy the sectors exactly as they are on the original disk. **copy *.***, on the other hand, will find all the parts of a file on the source disk and record them in a nice contiguous file on the target disk. It's a good reorganization to do when you suspect things are getting a bit disjointed on the original disk.

Try it. With the default set to B>, with a formatted disk in Drive A and the sample disk in Drive B, type:

copy *.* a: [ENTER]

One-Drive SYSTEM

It will be necessary to fool the computer again. Your command is the same as above, except that your Sample disk is in Drive A, so type the command **copy *.* b:** [ENTER]. You'll be prompted to switch disks back and forth until the copying is complete.

., by the way, is usually pronounced "star dot star."

Deleting Files Using the Wildcard

When a particular project is finished and you want to clean up the disk, a whole series of similar files can be deleted using the wildcard and the **del** command. At the B> prompt, type:

del howdy.* [ENTER]

...and check the directory. All three HOWDYs will be gone. Next type:

del *.dog [ENTER] to remove all the .DOG files. Leave the .CAT files for the next chapter.

Any individual file can be deleted with the **del** command by simply following the command with the file's full name.

Using the ? Wildcard

The ? can be used to replace a single letter. If for instance you were looking for a file named FRANCES2, and you couldn't remember if it was spelled FRANCES or FRANCIS, you could type: **dir franc?s2**. In this particular case, the * wildcard would have been less precise, because the * replaces everything that follows, whereas the ? only replaces a single letter. While **dir franc*** would have found FRANCES2 for you, it would also have found FRANCES3, FRANCES4 and so on.

SUMMARY

* MS-DOS assumes the default drive. If no drive designation is specified with a file name, MS-DOS looks on the default drive.
* In a copy operation, if no new file name is given, MS-DOS will give the new file the same name as the old.
* To change the default drive from A to B, type **b:** [ENTER]
* If the MS-DOS disk is in Drive A and the default has been changed to B, type **path a:** [ENTER] to permit use of external commands.
* The * wildcard takes the place of file names or extensions. It can also be used if only part of the filename is known. Example: GREET* for GREETING.
* The * wildcard can be substituted for *both* file names and extensions. To copy all files, *.* is used.
* The ? wildcard takes the place of an individual character. Example: FRANC?S for FRANCES or FRANCIS.

Creating More Sample Files

We've talked about how the **copy** command makes duplicate files on the same disk and on a different disk, but we're not finished with **copy** yet. There are a number of other things it can do. For example, it can be used to copy from the *console* to the disk. That means that you can type a document on the keyboard, then save it to the disk as a file. No need to go into BASIC or your word processor or anything else. Just type and save. This is no substitute for a word processor, mind you, but it's good for a quick note and will serve for creating a few more sample files.

Sample File 1 - NAMELIST

The **copy** command is used the same way we used it before; **copy** *source* to *destination*. The source in this case will be the console because you'll be typing the text in at the keyboard. The destination will be the drive and file name you want it saved to. With a formatted disk in Drive B and the A> prompt on the screen (return to it if you're not already there), try this one:

copy con b:namelist [ENTER]
Winston Churchill [ENTER]
William Shakespeare [ENTER]
Jacques Cousteau [ENTER]
Elizabeth Taylor [ENTER]
Fred Flintstone [ENTER]

To tell MS-DOS you're finished, press $\boxed{\text{CTRL}}$ $\boxed{\text{Z}}$ (hold down the $\boxed{\text{CTRL}}$ key and press $\boxed{\text{Z}}$) or just press $\boxed{\text{F6}}$. This will appear at the bottom of your list:

^Z

Press $\boxed{\text{ENTER}}$ again and NAMELIST is recorded on the data disk. Check the directory to verify.

Single Drive Systems
The **copy** command does not require the MS-DOS disk to be in place. Put the data disk in the drive, and don't specify a drive designation when typing the file name.

Sample File 2 · NOTE

Let's type a little note to go with the list of names. Call this one NOTE:

copy con b:note $\boxed{\text{ENTER}}$
Dear Barbara, $\boxed{\text{ENTER}}$
Here is the list of people I've invited to the party. $\boxed{\text{ENTER}}$
Hope they can all come. $\boxed{\text{ENTER}}$
$\boxed{\text{ENTER}}$
J.K. $\boxed{\text{ENTER}}$
$\boxed{\text{ENTER}}$
^Z $\boxed{\text{ENTER}}$

As you can see, the $\boxed{\text{ENTER}}$ key is not there just to make things happen in MS-DOS; it also functions as the "carriage return" when you're typing more than one line. (If you're wondering about that extra $\boxed{\text{ENTER}}$ between the signature and the ^Z, it's for something we have up our sleeve for a future chapter...)

Limitations

If you've used a word processor, you know that it makes great things possible when it comes to editing and moving text around. A good word processor is to a typewriter approximately what a Maserati is to a pogo stick. **copy con,**

when used to create text files, fits into that spectrum somewhere in the
"moped" area. It gets you there, if you're not in a hurry, but no frills.

Don't expect, for example, *wraparound*--the ability to determine that the last
word on the line won't fit and automatically drop it to the next line. There'll
be no inserting of text in the middle of a line or even overstriking correct
letters over wrong ones. When you get as close to the end of the line as you
dare, you must press ENTER. If you make a mistake, the BACKSPACE or ←
key erases as the cursor backs up. Type the text over, hopefully correctly this
time.

MS-DOS does have a text editor called EDLIN. We'll be looking at it in
Chapter 25.

Displaying Files

You've used MS-DOS like a typewriter to create some new files; to retrieve
and look at them, use the **type** command. First check the directory to verify
their exact names and to make sure they're actually there. Pick one you'd like
to see and type:

type b:namelist ENTER

There's the list. Try the same thing with NOTE. The **type** command is
primarily used to view data files--those plain-English files created by you. If
you'd like to see what happens when you try to use **type** to read machine-
language files, try it on FORMAT.COM on the MS-DOS disk. An interesting
display, but not very usable.

BASIC files, as well as data files created by other application programs, can
generally be read with **type**, but they will contain some odd-looking characters
and won't be formatted the way you'd see them if you had the application
program up and running. **type** is a good quick check, when you're looking
through a directory at MS-DOS level, to determine whether a file is the one
you're thinking of or not.

SUMMARY

* Type **copy con** <**file name**> to create files from the keyboard.
* End the file with [CTRL] [Z] or [F6] (displays ^Z).
* **copy con** does not do wraparound or permit editing.
* Use EDLIN (Chapter 25) for more advanced capabilities.
* Use **type** <**file name**> to view a text file currently stored on disk.

CHAPTER 20

Combining Files

Combining files is another **copy** command trick. You may, for example, decide that one of your word processor files should be added onto the end of another. Or when you get to Volume 2 and start working with *batch files*, you may elect to combine one series of commands with another. Whatever the reason, combining files is as simple as the following example. To avoid the necessity of adding the **b:** drive designator each time, either change the default drive to ᴮ⟩, or put your data disk in Drive A. Type:

copy note + namelist party [ENTER]

You've just told MS-DOS to add NAMELIST to NOTE and combine them into a file called PARTY. Both NOTE and NAMELIST still exist, but now there is a new file which contains them both. Look at it with the **type** command:

type party [ENTER]

```
Dear Barbara,
Here is the list of people I've invited to the party.
Hope they can all come.

J.K.

Winston Churchill
William Shakespeare
Jacques Cousteau
Elizabeth Taylor
Fred Flintstone
```

Note that if you had specified **NAMELIST** first in the **copy** command, the combined file (PARTY) would have begun with the list instead of the note. The extra [ENTER] we stuck in after the signature back in Chapter 19 was to provide the blank line between the files when they were combined. Without it, it would appear that the list of names began with J.K.

SUMMARY

* To combine two files, type **copy** <**first file name**> + <**second file name**> <**name of new file to contain both**> [ENTER].
* In the command, list the files in the order you want them to appear in the combined file.

CHAPTER 21

Printing Files

In Chapter 3, you learned how to print what was on the screen. There are a couple of ways to print files from the *disk*. The first and simplest is the all-purpose **copy** command.

Copying from a Disk to the Printer

You've already learned how to copy from the console to the disk (Chapter 19). In similar fashion, you can copy from the disk to the printer, simply by specifying the file as the source and the printer (**prn**) as the target. Try it with PARTY. Again, be sure to have the disk containing your text files in the default drive. Type:

copy party prn [ENTER]

PARTY goes directly to the printer, without ever appearing on the screen.

Copying from the Console to the Printer

Since it's possible to copy from the console to the disk and from the disk to the printer, why not copy from the console right to the printer? Why not? Type:

copy con prn [ENTER]

Now type something relevant:

"You are old, father William," the young man said,
"And your hair has become very white;
and yet you incessantly stand on your head -
Do you think, at your age, it is right?"

^Z [ENTER]

The [CTRL] [Z] tells the computer that the file is ended and ready for printing.
Pressing [ENTER] starts the printer.

Printing Files with the "Printing Queue"

When you need to print a number of files, and you don't want to wait for
them to finish before you can use the computer, you can stack them up in
a line, or "queue," to print automatically, while you do something else. It
will appear that the computer is doing two things at once, but what is actually
happening is a procedure called time sharing. When you're not actually typing
a character at the keyboard, the computer takes advantage of the pause, however brief, to go back to printing files.

You only have three text files on your disk so far, so to make the demonstration a little more impressive, let's print them each twice. The command
to print files in a print queue is simply **print**. As soon as you give the command, start typing something else--anything to demonstrate to yourself that
the computer truly isn't locked up during the printing operation; that it will
allow you to go about your business even though files are being fed to the
printer. This will become much more dramatic when you have long files of
your own to print later.

print note namelist party note namelist party

One-Drive SYSTEM

print is an *external* command, which means that the MS-DOS disk is
needed to get it going. All you do is specify that the text files are on the
imaginary Drive B. Put the MS-DOS disk in first and type:

print b:note b:namelist b:party b:note b:namelist b:party

You'll be prompted to insert the diskette for Drive B, which is your data
disk. Once it's in, press any key and printing will begin.

Once printing starts, the message on the screen tells you that:

```
B:PARTY    ,        is currently being printed
B:NAMELIST,         is in queue
B:NOTE     ,        is in queue
B:PARTY    ,        is in queue
B:NAMELIST,         is in queue
B:NOTE     ,        is in queue
```

You will notice that each file is printed on a separate sheet of paper. The ^Z,
called the *end of file marker*, causes the printer to feed a new sheet so your
files don't all run together. Of course, if you don't have a continuous-feed
printer, you'll have to put in a new sheet for each file.

Adding to the Print Queue

Up to ten files can be in the queue at any one time. In the event your list
of files exceeds that number, you can add on to the end of the queue as the
first files are completed. Suppose, for example, you had fifteen files named
ONE through FIFTEEN. Only files ONE through TEN could go into the
queue to start with, but once the first five were printed, you could add in the
five that wouldn't fit using the following form of the **print** command:

print eleven/p twelve thirteen fourteen fifteen

See the **/p** after the first file name? That's the signal to add these names to the queue. The /p affects the name immediately preceding it *and all names that follow*.

Removing (Cancelling) Files from the Print Queue

If, in the above example, you got printing started and then changed your mind about files EIGHT, NINE, and TEN, give the cancel command:

print eight/c nine ten

Again, the **/c** goes after the first name in the cancellation list, and ahead of all others that are to be taken out of the queue.

Terminating the Print Queue

To terminate the whole deal and cancel the queue altogether, type:

print /t

SUMMARY

---

* To print a file from the disk, type **copy** <**file name**> **prn** [ENTER].
* To print directly from the keyboard, first type **copy con prn** [ENTER]. Then type your text. Each line will be printed when [ENTER] is pressed at the end of the line. End the job with [CTRL] [Z] [ENTER].
* To print a number of files (printing queue), type **print** <**file name**> <**file name**> <**file name**> ...etc. [ENTER].
* To add to the print queue, include **/p** following the first file name in the list of files to be added. Example: **print eleven/p twelve thirteen** ...etc. [ENTER].
* To remove (cancel) files from the print queue, include **/c** following the first file name in the list of files to be cancelled. Example: **print eight/c nine ten** ...etc. [ENTER].
* To terminate the entire print queue, type **print/t** [ENTER].

CHAPTER 22

Renaming Files

When you create files with MS-DOS or an application program, you will probably assign names to them on a more-or-less spur of the moment basis. If you use MS-DOS to keep things organized by keeping a close eye on the directories, deleting extraneous files, copying, combining and so on, you will also want to do some renaming. You may, for example, end up with a set of files named BUDGET, BUDGET.JUL, BGT.JUN, APRIL.BGT, MAYBGT.DAT, and a few other variations as a result of forgetting, in one month, what you used in previous months. Or you may have a few sets of hands in the pie, each with a personal style of naming files.

At reorganizing time, the **rename** command allows you to change your mind about what a file is named without copying it to a new file and deleting the old. The above examples could be changed, for instance, to BUDGET.APR, BUDGET.MAY, BUDGET.JUN and so on, so that they'd be orderly and all show up together on the directory. (More on this in Chapter 23). They'd be much easier to find and use. Try it on one of your sample files. At the B> prompt, type:

rename namelist names.txt [ENTER]

This changes NAMELIST to NAMES.TXT. The .TXT extension is a reminder to you that this is a text file, meaning simply that it is made up of words you can read. Some people label all their word processor and other text-type files this way. Files with the same name or extension, remember, can be handled as a group using the * wild card. We'll try that in a moment. Use **rename** to add the .TXT extension to your other two text files:

rename party party.txt [ENTER]

...or try it using the wildcard as a shortcut:

rename note *.txt [ENTER]

Using the * means "rename NOTE to the *same name* plus .TXT."

Renaming a Group of Files Using the Wildcard

Check the Directory to see that they've all been changed. Now try renaming a whole group of files using the wildcard:

rename *.txt *.dat [ENTER]

This example changes all files with the extension .TXT to files with the extension .DAT. The file names themselves won't change.

The wildcard can also take the place of the extension, of course; For example, if you had a group of files named BUDGET.MAY, BUDGET.JUN, BUDGET.JUL and so on, and wanted to change them to something like EXPENSES.MAY, EXPENSES.JUN etc., you would type:

rename budget.* expenses.* [ENTER]

SUMMARY
* To rename a file, type **rename** <**old name**> <**new name**> [ENTER].
* The * wildcard can be substituted for either the old name or the new when only the extension is to be changed. Example: **rename** <**old name**> ***.**< **new extension**> [ENTER]. This keeps the name the same but adds or changes the extension.
* The * wildcard can also be substituted for the extension.

CHAPTER 23

Sorting Files

Putting a Directory in Alphabetical Order

The order in which file names appear in a directory depends upon how the files were saved in the first place. If you write and save them one at a time, the name of each new file will usually be added to the bottom of the directory. As files are deleted and others added, the names in the directory will end up in no useful order whatever. The names can, however, be put in alphabetical order with the **sort** command.

In order to sort things, MS-DOS temporarily stores information on the MS-DOS disk, so its write-protect tab must be removed, even though the directory you're going to sort is on Drive B.

First put the directory of your data diskette up on the screen and take a look at it. Notice that the names of the files are not in any particular order. Now, with the A⟩ prompt on the screen, type:

dir b: ¦ **sort** ENTER

One-Drive Systems
Type the command just as above. You'll be prompted several times to switch back and forth between the disk you are sorting and the MS-DOS disk.

The vertical line between the drive designator and the **sort** command is called a *pipe*. It is located on the 4 key on the numeric keypad at the right side of the keyboard. To use it, the [NUM LOCK] key must be toggled off. If the light on [NUM LOCK] is lit, press it again to shut it off. (On the 1200 HD, the pipe is located to the left of the left [Shift] key.)

The Pipe

The pipe connects commands; it "pipes" the output of one command into the input of another. In the example above, you gave the command to go to the disk and fetch the directory. Instead of outputting that directory right to the screen as usual, MS-DOS sent it to the *sort filter*, a little program that takes what it receives and puts it in alpha or numeric order. After this brief detour, the directory finally made it to the screen.

The directory you just sorted does not stay sorted, however; that's not the intent of the **sort** command. It only displays a sorted output. Type **dir b:** and you'll see the directory in its regular, unsorted format. The output of a sort can be saved to a file so that it can be used later without having to sort again.

Sending Output of the Sort Command to a File with the >

The pipe (¦) sends the output of a command to another command. The *greater-than* symbol (>) sends the output to a file. Type:

dir b: ¦ **sort** > **b:dirfile** [ENTER]

This set of orders does the following:

1. calls up the directory of Drive B.
2. pipes it into the **sort** command.
3. arranges the directory in alphabetical order.
4. sends the sorted output to a file on Drive B called DIRFILE.

Notice that since you sent the directory to a file, it didn't go to the screen. If DIRFILE had existed, it would have been written over. Since it didn't, MS-DOS simply created the file.

Type **type b:dirfile** ENTER to see the permanently sorted copy of the directory. Caution: this is just a text file; it's not automatically updated each time there is a change in the *actual* directory.

Sending Output of the Sort Command to the Printer with the >

When the **sort** program finishes with the directory, it has to send it somewhere. If you don't specify, it automatically goes to the console (screen). Adding a file name after the > sends it to a file, and adding **prn** after the > sends it to the printer. Type:

dir b: ¦ **sort** > **prn** ENTER

This time, you explain what each part of the above command did.

Sorting on Other Columns

Sorting the way you have just done puts the output in alpha or numeric order sorted on the first letter of each line. The first letter of each line is called *column one*. The second letters form vertical column two, and so on. Suppose you wanted the output of this directory sorted in such a way that all the .BAS files were together and all the .TXT files were together. The simplest way to achieve this would be to arrange the file names so that their extensions are in alphabetical order. Put the directory back up on the screen and count over to the beginning of the file name extensions. The longest name (GREETING) has the maximum of eight characters, and there is one space between those long names and their extensions, so all the extensions must begin in column ten, right? Count for yourself. To sort by extension (column ten), type:

dir b: ¦ **sort** /+10 ENTER

To sort on file size, count over to the end of the extensions, plus one space, and you're in column 14. This is where the next area, file size, actually begins. Type:

dir b: ¦ **sort** /+14 ENTER

Since column 14 contains numerical data, the sort is in increasing numerical order.

Reverse Order Sorting with /r

Descending order, either alpha or numeric, requires the addition of **/r** to the **sort** command. The **/r** goes in front of the column number. Type:

dir b: ┊ sort /r/ + 14 [ENTER]

Sorting a File

We've been using the directory of Drive B as an example, but directories are not the only thing that can be sorted. The **sort** command can be extremely useful for organizing files which contain lists, providing the list is columnar or the first letter in each line is the one to be sorted. Examples:

Winston	Churchill
William	Shakespeare
Jacques	Cousteau
Elizabeth	Taylor
Fred	Flintstone

Arranging the file this way requires the use of the [TAB] key when creating the file. Two tabs after the shorter names and one tab after Elizabeth line all last names up in column 17, so they can be sorted. Here's another approach:

Churchill, Winston
Shakespeare, William
Cousteau, Jacques
Taylor, Elizabeth
Flintstone, Fred

This arrangement starts the last names in column 1, again making them easy to sort. Let's try the second example. Open a new sample file called NEWLIST. Remember how?

copy con b:newlist [ENTER]

...and type the list, last name first, as above. Don't forget the ˆ**Z** [ENTER] at the end.

Once the new file is created, sorting it requires this form of the **sort** command:

sort < b:newlist [ENTER]

Notice there is no pipe this time. The reason is that there is only one command: **sort**. We used the > to send *output* to a file a moment ago; this time we're using the < (less-than) to obtain *input* to the sort filter from the file named NEWLIST. NEWLIST appears on the screen with the last names in alphabetical order. How about sorting a file and saving the result as a new file?

Saving the Contents of a Sorted File

If you think about this one, you can probably guess how to do it:

sort < b:newlist > b:lastname [ENTER]

This time, we sorted using input from NEWLIST and sent the output to a file called LASTNAME. Since the file didn't previously exist, it was specially created for the occasion. Again, output went to the new file, not to the screen. Output could also have been directed to the screen, instead of a file, the same way we did it with the directory.

SUMMARY

* To sort a directory, type **dir <drive designation>** ¦ **sort** [ENTER].
* The ¦ (pipe) is on the [4] key on the ten-key pad. [NUM LOCK] must be off.
* To send output of the **sort** command to a file, add > and the file name to the end of the sort command.
* To send output of the **sort** command to the printer, add > and **prn** to the end of the **sort** command.
* To sort on columns other than the first, add /+ and the column number to the end of the **sort** command.
* To sort in reverse alpha or numeric order, add /r to the end of the **sort** command. If sorting on a column, add /+ and the column number *after* the /r. Example: **dir b:** ¦ **sort /r/+14** [ENTER].
* To sort a text file, type **sort** < and the file name [ENTER].

* To save the contents of a sorted file, type **sort** < **(old file name)** > **(new file name)** [ENTER]. This sorts the contents of the old file, and saves the sorted contents to a new file.

CHAPTER 24

Searching Files

Searching a Directory

In the last chapter, you made a little more sense out of the directory by putting it in alphabetical or numeric order. As your directories grow, even this may not be enough to allow you to find what you're looking for quickly. In Chapter 18, you searched through the directory for specific file names by simply typing **dir** and the name, or **dir** and a partial name, along with a wild card.

The **find** command will search for any group of characters. For example, you remember that you put on the disk a couple of files that contained names. You can't remember anything about the file names except that they probably included the letters NAME. The files could be called MYNAME85, NEW-NAME2, THE$NAME or who knows what.

In order to search through a directory, you first have to give the **dir** command, then "pipe in" the **find** command--just as you did in the last chapter with **sort**. To find the *character string* NAME in the directory of Drive B, type:

dir b: ¦ **find "NAME"** [ENTER]

A couple of things to notice in this command: the string to be searched for must be in quotes, and capitalization must be exactly as it appears in the directory. We give most of our commands to MS-DOS in lowercase, even though it will accept both lower and uppercase. In the directory, however, MS-DOS converts all file names to uppercase, so to look for a file name, you have to use uppercase. The screen displays two file names containing NAME:

```
NAMES     DAT       75    10-03-85   12:34a
LASTNAME            95    10-04-85   10:15a
```

Your dates and times will of course be different.

Searching a Text File

The real benefit of the **find** command is in searching through your text files. Searching a file does not require the pipe and does not require you to be in the file already. For example, with the B> prompt on the screen (A>, if you have only one drive), search through NEWLIST for the name Winston:

find "Winston" newlist [ENTER]

First you told it to find, then what to find, and finally where to find it. Notice that Winston has a capital W in the command, because that's how it occurs in the file. If you're not sure if a word will be capitalized in the file, simply leave out the first letter altogether; in this case, search for "inston".

```
------------ newlist
Churchill, Winston
```

The entire line is displayed; not just the search string. That's why it's okay to leave out part of the word. Try this next:

find "Wi" newlist.txt [ENTER]

This time it found two lines in the file that contained the requested string:

```
------------ newlist
Churchill, Winston
Shakespeare, William
```

Requesting the Line Number of the Searched-for String

Once MS-DOS has proved to you that the string does indeed exist in your file, what good does it do you? If you want to change something in the string, you have to open up the file and then you're faced with the problem of finding the string all over again. The **find** command will help out by telling you exactly what line the string is on. Then you can go into the file using the MS-DOS editor (*EDLIN*--coming up in the next chapter) and scan through the lines by number to make the repair.

Let's look for Elizabeth Taylor. Type:

find/n "liz" newlist ENTER

And the computer responds with:

```
------------ newlist
[4]Taylor, Elizabeth
```

find/n means, "Find it and give its line number." In the next chapter, we'll take that bit of information and do something with it.

Finding All Lines That *Do Not* Contain the String

Another extension to the **find** command makes it possible to find all entries in the NEWLIST file that do not contain the string "Wi", type:

find/v "Wi" newlist ENTER

The **/v** causes the find filter to "filter out" the string, displaying all other lines.

```
------------ newlist
Cousteau, Jacques
Taylor, Elizabeth
Flintstone, Fred
```

Counting the Number of Times the String Occurs

The last option available is /c. This extension doesn't display the string, it just counts the number of times it appears in the file and reports the count. Since these **find** features can be used with directories, let's search the directory of the MS-DOS disk for something we can find in a large enough quantity to be semi-impressive. How about the file name extension COM? Don't forget the pipe:

dir a: ¦ find/c "COM" [ENTER]

Because you've changed the default drive to B⟩ for convenience in working with the data disk, it is necessary to specify the drive designation when asking for the directory of Drive A. As long as B is the default drive, MS-DOS automatically looks there, unless otherwise instructed.

Combining Two Find Features

There are three extensions to the **find** command: /n which gives line number, /v which displays all lines that do not contain the string and /c which just counts. The /v and /n features ("parameters") can be used together. Do not combine /c with either of them. Try this:

find/n /v "Wi" namelist [ENTER]

And there are the three entries that *don't* contain "Wi", complete with their line numbers:

```
----------- namelist
[3]Cousteau, Jacques
[4]Taylor, Elizabeth
[5]Flintstone, Fred
```

SUMMARY

* When searching directories or files, drive designations are not required if searched files are on the default drive.
* To search a directory, type **dir ¦ find "<character string>"** [ENTER].

* To search a text file, type **find "<character string>" <file name>** [ENTER].
* Capitalization must be identical to the occurrence of the string in the file. If uncertain about capitalization of first letter in word, leave first letter out.
* If uncertain of spelling of string, search for part of it.
* To obtain line number of string, type **find/n "<character string>" <file name>** [ENTER].
* To find all lines that do *not* contain the string, type **find/v "<character string>" <file name>** [ENTER].
* To count the number of times a string occurs, type **find/c "<character string>" <file name>** [ENTER].
* The **find** command can have both the **/n and /v** extensions at the same time. The **/c** extension cannot be combined with either of the other two.

CHAPTER 25

Edlin: The MS-DOS Text Editor

Edlin (for 'edit line') is a very useful "accessory" program included with MS-DOS. As we mentioned earlier, the ultimate textmaking machine is a good word processor. We offered the opinion that the spectrum ran something like this:

* A good word processor (like SCRIPSIT) = exotic sportscar.
* The MS-DOS **copy con** command = motorized bicycle.
* A typewriter = pogo stick.

If we may carry this little exaggeration one step further, we would probably call Edlin a Volkswagen Beetle; simple, compact and all some users will ever need, but short on luxuries. We won't attempt to provide a complete course in Edlin in this introductory book, but we'll give you a quick overview. Volume 2 covers the subject in full detail.

Creating a New File with Edlin

The first order of business is loading the Edlin program and naming the file you want to create. Type:

edlin jack.ltr [ENTER]

Edlin responds with:

```
New file
*
```

Like BASIC, Edlin is a self-contained program and therefore uses its own prompt (the *). As long as you're in Edlin, you won't see the familiar A⟩ or B⟩ system prompts. The * means the same thing and reminds you that you're in Edlin where only Edlin commands will work and other MS-DOS commands are not available.

The first Edlin command you'll need is the 'insert text' command which is simply the letter **i**.

*i [ENTER]

Given the insert command, Edlin responds with:

    1:*

Every line in an Edlin file has a number. The number is for use on the screen only: it doesn't become part of the text and won't show up when the file is printed out. The prompt is at line number 1, so let's type some text:

1:*Dear Jack, [ENTER]
2:*Sorry you couldn't make it to the party last night. [ENTER]
3:*You missed Liz Taylor, Winston Churchill, Fred Flintstone, [ENTER]
4:*and Jacques Cousteau. [ENTER]
5:*Your Pal, [ENTER]
6:*JK [ENTER]
7:*[CTRL] [C]

Pressing [CTRL] [C] tells Edlin that you've reached the end of your message.

You must watch the screen when you're using Edlin, and press [ENTER] at the end of the last word you think you can get on each line. While it is possible to put up to 253 characters in each numbered "line," Edlin does not provide the *word-wrap* feature most word processors include. Word wrap moves the whole word down to the beginning of the next line if it won't fit on the previous line. Edlin will take a full 80 characters on one line, then drop to the next, even if it's in the middle of a word.

Inserting Text into a Line

If you were observant, you noticed we left a name out of our list. William Shakespeare was on the party list, but was not mentioned in this note to Jack. An unfortunate oversight, but easily remedied. To get back into a line in the current file, simply type its number and press [ENTER]. The logical place for Shakespeare's name is at the beginning of line 4. Type:

4 [ENTER]

Line 4 appears in its existing form, along with a second 4:* directly underneath, suggesting the opportunity to make some changes. You don't want to retype the whole line, however; you just want to insert a name. Press the [INSERT] key once ([Ins] on the 1200 HD). Now type **William Shakespeare**, and press the [INSERT] key again. What you just did was switch on the insert mode, type some new text and shut the insert mode off.

Now, what about the rest of the line? Hold down the [→] key and watch it magically appear before your eyes:

4:*William Shakespeare and Jacques Cousteau,

Press [ENTER]. Would you like to see an even quicker way? Press [4] [ENTER] again to open up line 4. Press the [INSERT] key and type:

Mr. and Mrs. (Leave a space after **Mrs.**)

Press [INSERT] again and then press the [F3] key. Zip! There's the rest of the line. Press [ENTER] to complete the editing of line 4, and type **1l** (the number one and a lowercase letter l) and [ENTER]. This tells Edlin to start with line 1 and list (display) the entire file. It now reads:

1: Dear Jack,
2: Sorry you couldn't make it to the party last night,
3: You missed Liz Taylor, Winston Churchill, Fred Flintstone,
4: *Mr, and Mrs, William Shakespeare and Jacques Cousteau,
5: Your Pal,
6: JK

The * in front of the contents in Line 4 indicates that 4 was the last active line. What you've actually been doing in editing this line is replacing the original line 4 with a new one. When you typed **4** and the original line appeared along with another 4:*, MS-DOS was telling you "Anything you put on this new line 4 will replace the original. You can insert things with the INSERT key, accept what was there by tapping the → or F3 keys, or delete things, but whatever form the line has when you finish and press ENTER is what will go into the file."

Deleting Text from a Line

On second thought, it does seem a bit ludicrous to suggest that Mr. and Mrs. Shakespeare were there (he wasn't even married, was he?). To delete everything up to a certain letter, use the F4 key. In this case, you want to delete Mr. and Mrs., which is everything up to the W in William. Press 4 ENTER to put line 4 back up on the screen, then do this:

F4 SHIFT W F3 ENTER

The F4 told Edlin to delete everything up to the specified character, which was a capital W (designed by pressing SHIFT W), and F3 caused it to retype the rest of the existing line. ENTER finished the editing job. Typing **1l** ENTER displays the file in its latest form, without the Mr. and Mrs.

Changing Your Mind

Press 5 ENTER , then the → key to move past the word Your and type **Friend,** where Pal, used to be. Before pressing ENTER , change your mind and decide to leave Pal as it was. To undo a change before you press ENTER , use the ESC (Escape) key. Just press it once and the line will look like this:

5:*Your Friend,\

The backslash indicates that this new version of the line has been cancelled. Now press ENTER and list the File with **1l** and see that Your Pal, is just as it was.

Printing an Edlin File

Printing an Edlin file is no more difficult than printing any other MS-DOS file. Be sure your printer is hooked up and turned on, then simply press the PRINT key (Ctrl Prt Sc on the 1200 HD) once to tell MS-DOS that you want it to print what follows. List the file with **1l**, and as each line appears on the screen, it will be printed.

Ending the Editing

There are two ways to finish up an editing job: Pressing Q ENTER at the * prompt quits editing but does not save any changes you have made since the last time the file was saved on the disk. A message appears asking you if you're sure you want to do that. Press N ENTER .

Pressing E ENTER at the * prompt ends the editing, saves the file to the disk in its new form, and exits Edlin. Press E ENTER .

There is much more to Edlin waiting for you in Volume 2, but you now know how to open a file, make insertions and deletions to it, print it and get back out of Edlin. That should be enough of a taste to help you decide if you are interested in going on with it.

SUMMARY

* To open Edlin and start a new file, type **edlin <file name>** ENTER .
* The prompt for Edlin is *.
* To insert text, type **i** ENTER .
* To end a file created in Edlin, press CTRL C .
* To edit a line, just type its line number and ENTER .
* To insert within a line, use the arrow keys to move to the desired place, press the INSERT key once, type the new text and press INSERT again.
* To delete everything up to a certain character, type the line number to put the line on the screen, then press F4 , the character, and ENTER .
* To display the rest of the line, after an insertion or deletion, press F3 .
* To cancel a change before pressing ENTER , press ESC .
* To print an Edlin file, press PRINT , then list the file with **1l** ENTER .
* Pressing Q ENTER at the * prompt quits Edlin but does not save changes.
* Pressing E ENTER at the * prompt quits Edlin and saves the edited file to disk.

CHAPTER 26

Review of Part Three

Part Three has been an introduction to the MS-DOS commands that are used to handle your files. Files created using MS-DOS or the MS-DOS editor (Edlin) as well as files created with BASIC or application software can be manipulated with these commands.

Commands

b: or **c:**, etc. changes the default drive.

BASIC

BASIC loads the BASIC programming language.
    LIST or [F1] displays a BASIC program.
    RUN or [F2] runs a BASIC program.
    LOAD or [F3] loads a BASIC program from disk into memory.
    SAVE or [F4] saves a BASIC program to disk.
    NEW clears the current BASIC program out of memory.
    SYSTEM exits BASIC and returns to MS-DOS.

Path

path a: causes MS-DOS to search for command programs on Drive A when A is not the default drive.

Copy

copy oldfile newfile creates a duplicate file on the same disk. Different file names must be used (OLDFILE and NEWFILE are sample file names.)

copy a:somefile b:somefile creates a duplicate file on a disk in a different drive. Drive designator must be included with at least one file name. The file names can be identical. (SOMEFILE is sample name.)

copy somefile b: is a short cut for creating a duplicate file with the same name on a different disk.

copy con somefile creates files from the keyboard.
End file with [CTRL] [Z] [ENTER].

copy 1stfile + 2ndfile 3rdfile combines 1STFILE with 2NDFILE to create 3RDFILE.

copy somefile prn sends the file SOMEFILE from the disk to the printer.

copy con prn sends output of keyboard directly to printer.

Send the file to the printer with [CTRL] [Z] [ENTER].

Type

type somefile displays the file SOMEFILE on the screen from the disk.

Print (1stfile, 2ndfile etc. are sample file names)

print 1stfile 2ndfile 3rdfile...etc. prints series of files in a *print queue.*

    print 4thfile/p 5thfile 6thfile adds files to the queue.
    print 3rdfile/c 6thfile cancels files from the print queue.
    print/t terminates the print queue.

Rename

rename oldfile newfile changes name of OLDFILE to NEWFILE.

Sort

dir a: ⫶ **sort** sorts directory of Drive A.

> Adding > and a file name to the end of the command sends output of the sort to that file.
> Adding > and **prn** to the end of the command sends output of the sort to the printer.
> Adding **/+** and a column number to the end of the command sorts on a column other than column one.
> Adding **/r** to the end of the command sorts in reverse alpha or numeric order.

sort < **somefile** sorts a text file named SOMEFILE.

sort < **oldfile** > newfile sorts contents of OLDFILE and saves sorted text in NEWFILE.

Find

dir ⫶ **find "Fred"** searches for the word Fred in a directory.

find "Fred" somefile searches for Fred in a text file named SOMEFILE.

find /n "Fred" somefile obtains the number of the line that contains Fred in SOMEFILE.

find /v "Fred" somefile finds all lines that do not contain Fred in the file SOMEFILE.

find /c "Fred" somefile counts the number of times Fred occurs in SOMEFILE.

find/n and **find/v** can be combined into **find/n /v**.

Edlin

edlin somefile opens Edlin and creates a new or opens an existing file named SOMEFILE.

i inserts text.

[CTRL] [C] ends an Edlin file.

[INSERT] toggles insert mode on and off.

[F4] <character> deletes everything up to that character.

[F3] after an insertion or deletion displays rest of line.

[ESC] cancels a change in a line if pressed before [ENTER].

[PRINT] **1l** (the number 1 and a lower case letter l) prints an Edlin file on the screen.

[Q] at the * prompt quits Edlin but does not save changes.

[E] at the * prompt quits Edlin and saves the edited file to disk.

Index